Praise

THE
BOARDROOM
Entrepreneur

'A roadmap for employees who seek to unleash their entrepreneurial spirit in the workplace for the benefit of the company as a whole. Its theme, the need to harness latent innovative talent, makes it a relevant read at every level of an organisation'
Karan Bilimoria, founder and CEO, Cobra Beer

'Great book – brings the Beermat entrepreneurial energy to big business'
Sahar Hashemi, co-founder, Coffee Republic, and author of *Anyone Can Do It*

'Clear-headed, practical, profound'
Chris Nichols, Ashridge

'Everyone says "be more entrepreneurial" – but how do you do this, in a large organisation with preset goals and strategies? *The Boardroom Entrepreneur* shows the way'
John Barnes, Chairman, Harry Ramsden's, and co-author of *Marketing Judo*

'Understands the needs of bright employees and of the people who lead them'
David Taylor, author of *The Naked Leader* and *The Naked Leader Experience*

'If you're kicking your heels in a large organization, read this book and start stirring things up'
Jason Porter, co-founder, Friends Reunited

'Speaks a lot of common sense in a well-structured way'
Simon Woodroffe, Founder, Yo! Sushi

'Valuable reading for entrepreneur and corporate manager alike'
Bill Samuel, Director, Foyles

'The advertising and marketing industries are widely believed to be go-ahead and progressive, but can often fall foul of the usual corporate processes. *The Boardroom Entrepreneur* offers the key to unlocking enterprise again'
Bob Wootton, Director of Media and Advertising, ISBA

THE
BOARDROOM
Entrepreneur

Putting the craft of entrepreneurship
to work inside the large organisation

Mike Southon
& Chris West

Authors of
The Beermat Entrepreneur

To Lisa!
Keep the ideas coming!
Mike Southon

RANDOM HOUSE
BUSINESS BOOKS

Published by Random House Business Books 2005

2 4 6 8 10 9 7 3 5 1

Copyright © Mike Southon and Chris West 2005

Mike Southon and Chris West have asserted their right under the
Copyright, Designs and Patents Act, 1988 to be identified as the authors
of this work

Inserts on pages 56–59 and 127–128 are based on material previously
published in *Director* magazine written by the authors

First published in Great Britain in 2005 by
Random House Business Books
Random House, 20 Vauxhall Bridge Road, London SW1V 2SA

Random House Australia (Pty) Limited
20 Alfred Street, Milsons Point, Sydney, New South Wales 2061, Australia

Random House New Zealand Limited
18 Poland Road, Glenfield, Auckland 10, New Zealand

Random House (Pty) Limited
Endulini, 5a Jubilee Road, Parktown 2193, South Africa

The Random House Group Limited Reg. No. 954009
www.randomhouse.co.uk

A CIP catalogue record for this book is available from the British Library

ISBN 1 8441 3818 6

Papers used by The Random House Group Limited are natural,
recyclable products made from wood grown in sustainable forests. The
manufacturing processes conform to the environmental regulations
of the country of origin

Typeset in Foundry Form Sans and Bembo

Design and make up by Roger Walker

Printed and bound in the United Kingdom by
Biddles Ltd, King's Lynn

Contents

Foreword

by Sir John Rose, CEO Rolls-Royce Group plc

 **Rolls-Royce**

Corporate renewal is always a timely topic. At Rolls-Royce we have been practising it for 100 years: when the first aeroplanes took to the skies; when Frank Whittle's jet engine needed to be turned from a prototype into a reliable, mass-produced product; when marine technology demanded a totally new kind of propulsion. We are still practising it as we go into the energy-conscious but energy-hungry 21st century.

Yet there is also a need for continuity. Market booms come and go: solid businesses have to retain their knowledge, their traditions, their values and their 'core competencies'. We are always aware of this need for balance.

Mike and Chris understand this perfectly. They bring to the corporate context the vigour and imagination of entrepreneurs, without wishing to swamp the existing culture and business. They understand that, although corporate renewal must be shaped by the fast-changing marketplace, the driving force of it must lie in the company's *existing* people, in their passion, talent, originality and determination.

They also make the process fun, but practical and results-driven, never a detour into fantasy.

I recommend this entertaining and thoughtful book to all management concerned to balance the demands of innovation and stability, in search of ways of motivating and retaining bright individuals, and eager to make a difference to their companies and to the world around them.

Sir John Rose, Derby, 2004

Authors' note

Many people have helped with this book. We would
particularly like to thank Peter Wilson, Henri Winand, Chris
Nichols and Jeanette Kehoe, both for top-class theoretical input
and for letting us trial and develop our ideas in their
organisations. Many other people have helped via general
conversations or with specific information: Lucy Armstrong,
Graham Beswick, Jeromy Bird, Mark Clement, Keith
Haviland, Graham Michelli, Abe Peled, Rupert Sebag-
Montefiore, Bob Wootton – and, of course, our wives,
Virginia and Rayna, who have discussed this material with us
more than anyone. Thanks also to our agent, David Grossman,
for helping us navigate the choppy waters of the publishing
world, and to the excellent team at Random House, the fine
port where we have ended up.

Mike Southon and Chris West,
London/Cambridge, 2004

Monday morning.

The alarm goes, appallingly early. As you pad down the stairs to make a cup of tea, you look round at the house and a vague feeling of unease comes over you. You ask yourself that dreadful question again: is it worth it?

Yes, of course it is. That's why you do what you do – work for a large organisation, with all the security that entails.

But does that work have to be so dull? After staring at the kitchen clock for a minute or so, you remember you forgot to switch the kettle on.

No, 'dull' is unfair. Work isn't dull, it's just restricted. Half the time you know you could do a better job, if only…

If only. Two painful words.

As you get the milk from the fridge, a new feeling comes over you: envy. Not of other people's wealth – you're doing fine, though a bit extra would always come in handy. No, it's their freedom. Other people don't have to keep muttering 'If only…'

The CEO, for example. She had that idea of setting up the online subsidiary. It happened. She had the idea of moving widget production to Guangdong Province. It happened. You have ideas too, good ones – and what happens? Two more painful words. Damn all.

★   ★   ★

At the same time, the object of this envy has been up for an hour. The CEO is sitting in her chauffeur-driven car, catching up on some research. Want to hear something to cheer you up? She is worried, too. It wasn't that long ago that she promised the City 'double-digit growth'. OK, that was in the boom time – but right now, those double digits are 0.0. Some of that is due to write-offs, but the real problem is the core businesses. They are hardly growing at all. And why should they? The company operates in mature markets – that's why it's so big and so safe. Markets like that don't have real growth of 10 per cent per annum. Why should the participants?

Now, the City is losing patience. Spotty-faced analysts half her age have decided the CEO can't deliver. The share price is underperforming. Predators have even been seen circling round the business – if the underperformance continues, they'll gobble it up, strip out the bits they like and shut down the rest. And who will go down in history as the person who let that happen?

Most companies, she reflects, have a lifespan. Look at the facts… Of the original 500 components of the first (1957) Standard & Poor's Index, only 74 were still in the index in 1998, and of these only *two* had managed to outperform the index growth average over that period (and neither of them managed 'double-digit' growth). Furthermore, the rate of turnover has been accelerating, not just during the dot-com madness, but as a long-term trend.

Older indices tell an even sorrier story. Seventy years after the Forbes 100 was founded, more than 60 per cent of the originals haven't just disappeared from the index, but from the face of the corporate earth, bankrupt or swallowed up.

As the company Lexus turns into the gates of Head Office, a security guard in a peaked cap nods deferentially, but the CEO is far from happy.

Where can she get this growth from?

Incrementalism? Cutting costs, speeding things up, improving quality, gnawing away at rivals' market share… There is always room for this, especially if you ask the people who know where to find incremental improvement opportunities: people on the shop floor, sales reps, project engineers. In contrast to many change-gurus who despise incrementalism, this book will embrace it. But it cannot be the whole story: however good this CEO's incrementalist skills, she will be hard pressed to create £500 million of annual profits growth by these methods alone. In a mature marketplace, in this era of already flattened organisations, assumed 'Six Sigma quality' and universal information technology excellence…

Mergers and acquisitions? Every year another major survey appears bearing the same news: M and A doesn't create shareholder value. In most cases (the figure seems to vary from 50 to 80 per cent) shareholders actually lose. It's a horrible experience, too, wrecking morale with huge layoffs, vicious culture clashes and more backstabbing than a weekend with Cesare and Lucrezia Borgia. Quite why these surveys make news is a mystery – one day a survey will show that M and A creates value. Now that will be news.

True, some companies seem to be able to pull it off – Cisco and GE spring to mind – but the vast majority don't. Our CEO is wise to shake her head whenever bankers get on the phone with a potential merger target.

Creative accountancy? Worked well for Enron! However, this CEO would rather stay out of jail…

Going global? Selling to global markets and sourcing globally have created massive corporate success – OK, and a few disasters. But this is hardly new: ask anyone with green hair and they'll tell you it's been going on for years. Top companies are already globalising well. Is there potential for 'locked-in advantage' here? Actually, the answer may be 'yes' – but only if the company approaches the matter in a certain, radical way, which we will discuss later.

So is there a clearer way forward?

We believe the answer is 'yes'. Through what all businesses should do, and what the founders of her business – and of every other great business – did instinctively. **Innovation**.

The CEO has heard this before, too.

Innovation, like breaking up, is hard to do. To mark the millennium, the company had a huge innovation programme. Consultants in ponytails terrified the life out of established managers. They stuck posters in reception with quotes like 'If you're not part of the solution, you're part of the problem', and set up a series of trailblazing radical dot-com businesses that attracted huge media attention – and were later closed down, as quietly as possible, having lost millions of pounds. Around the same time the company also set up a corporate venturing arm, which is now the proud owner of a series of bankrupt ventures.

A better approach was clearly needed. Right now, a proposal for a highly structured Venture Initiative is sitting on the CEO's desk. The aim is to produce hundreds of business plans, which will then be subjected to lengthy and exhaustive analysis by committees of experts and highly paid consultants. The project is so expensive, in both money and time, that the Chief Financial Officer has threatened to resign if it is implemented. And at the same time the CEO has this nagging fear that it won't produce anything of value anyway. What was it her father used to say? 'Most new things don't work.'

Yet some new things do work, spectacularly well. Not long ago the house next door (the house just visible through the rhododendron bushes: the CEO lives in the nicest part of the nicest suburb of town) was sold to a successful entrepreneur. He has already added a conservatory and extended the garages to house his collection of Aston Martins.

The CEO couldn't care less about Aston Martins, but is worried about entrepreneurs. They get it right: big companies don't seem to. She's read all the books; she knows how, over and over again, big companies fail to innovate well, and how this usually happens not because they are stupid, but because they are clever. So clever that they know their existing business superbly, and are caught on the hop by change – discounting the clumsy, unfeasible, entrepreneurial alternatives in unprofitable sideline markets, which then suddenly metamorphose into superior substitutes for their mainstream products.

Could she become an entrepreneur, too, in the boardroom of a giant organisation?

She parks the Lexus next to the two-seater belonging to the HR director, who is at work even earlier: he has a whole load of things on his mind, too. Morale is not good, especially among the next generation of leaders, who seem in such a hurry...

The CEO walks slowly up the stone stairs with their worn 1960s handrail – how easy business seems to have been then – and into reception, remembering to smile: leaders, she knows, always have to be visible. Halfway to the lift she passes the bronze statue of the firm's Victorian founder, which was removed by the ponytail brigade as 'dangerous baggage from the past', and which has only recently been replaced. Sir Ernest made the first widgets in a rented workroom and delivered them to the local mills in a wheelbarrow. In those days, she muses, the company was flexible, imaginative, innovative, responsive…

We believe that it can be like this again, and that a return to those entrepreneurial roots is the way to bring that about. Not in the dot-com spirit of violent upheaval, but via a process of slower, but in the long run much more powerful, transformation. A quiet revolution.

Our previous book, *The Beermat Entrepreneur*, was – and still is, at time of writing – the UK's bestselling book on entrepreneurship. We wrote it as a reaction to the dot-com madness: that stuff was crazy; how do you really do entrepreneurship and create businesses that grow and last? We had many years' experience of start-ups, in good and bad eras, and we did plenty of research, meeting many entrepreneurs. After the book came out we met many more entrepreneurs, helping them with advice and contacts. We also talked to people in large organisations, and became convinced that entrepreneurship can and should be practised by them as well as by entrepreneurs. The question was: how, exactly? We read the literature; we talked more – to doubters as well as enthusiasts. We developed a philosophy and a method. We put them into practice, testing them against reality, rejecting bits that didn't work and building on the successes. The results follow.

We believe they can make the magic difference that the characters in the story above – the able but restless employee, the CEO, the HR Director – are all seeking.

What's in a name?

What is 'innovation'? Invention? Changing existing products? Quantum leaps in technology, like the motor car or the aeroplane? The answer, of course, is all of them. More clarity is needed.

Firstly, we believe it's worth preserving a distinction between **invention**, which is coming up with something new, and **innovation**, which is putting something new into commercial practice.

Secondly, we believe it is important to distinguish between **levels of innovation**. Of course this will be an oversimplification, but we much prefer having a few meaningful categories to the alternative of flapping our arms around and saying that it's all so complex that nobody can define anything – which is of course true in a very pure sense, but is not much use.

First comes **incremental innovation** – improvements to existing products, services, markets or processes. Obvious examples abound: a two-litre engine in a previously underpowered range of people carriers; a faster memory chip in a PC; that 'new, improved' washing powder; extending the warranty to include a free onsite visit by an engineer; opening an office in France; putting a 'blog' from the CEO on the intranet…

The next level is **step innovation**. This is a new category of product, or a new 'sub-technology'.

▶▶

Examples: the people carrier; replacing the 5¼ inch disk drive with the 3½ inch one in a PC; biological washing powder; putting warranties on things previously sold without them; entering the French market; setting up an intranet.

Above this comes what we call **revolutionary innovation**. When the mobs attacked Versailles palace, King Louis asked his first minister, 'Is this a revolt?' He got the grim reply, 'No, sire, it's a revolution.' Nothing was going to be the same again. Revolutionary innovation is that rare kind of change that has massive consequences, creating a whole range of new technologies, markets, manufacturing processes, business models, support networks, jobs and, ultimately, social institutions. Examples: the motor car; the PC; washing powder; the notion of after-sales service; exporting (the oldest revolutionary innovation we can think of!); the internet.

These distinctions aren't just academic. The resources needed for, and the consequences of, each kind of innovation are radically different.

Incremental innovation should be done almost by habit – but often isn't. Entrepreneurial attitudes play a major part in this important process. Later on we discuss a tested methodology for incrementalism.

Step innovation is a rougher ride, but with bigger potential rewards. It is probably this kind of innovation that this book is most aimed at producing. ▶▶

Revolutionary innovation is usually beyond the scope of any individual company – though anyone who takes a complex technology and masters the art of making it available to the mass market qualifies. Henry Ford is the classic example.

Note that you don't have to be a revolutionary innovator to create a dynamic, innovative business.

Finally, what do you call it when big organisations act entrepreneurially? Cynics say 'a miracle'. We disagree, but there is a lack of clarity. 'Corporate Venturing' is a nice term that captures the adventure of enterprise, but it is not used consistently: sometimes people use it to mean the specific activity whereby a company sets up a Venture Capital arm; at other times it is used more generally, for any kind of corporate enterprise. Disliking lack of clarity, we shall avoid it. There are also terms such as inventuring, imagineering (the term used at Disney Corp.) and 'internal business creation'. But the grandfather of corporate entrepreneurship, the American writer Gifford Pinchot, called it **'intrapreneurship'**. Original is best: we'll be using this term.

⸢Beermat.biz

Chapter One: The Right Stuff

We believe strongly that entrepreneurship is a *craft*: a range of skills united around a purpose. Much of this book is about this craft.

But entrepreneurship is about personality, too. At the heart of every successful enterprise is a human being with imagination, desire, courage, tenacity and shrewdness. The right stuff. Can these traits be acquired? Some people think so (see the box overleaf for a debate). We think not. And we celebrate that. Entrepreneurship is a talent, a calling.

What this does *not* mean is either: a) only entrepreneur types can be involved in enterprise, or b) once you have the right stuff, you don't need to learn anything. Wrong, on both counts. There are plenty of roles in the adventure of enterprise for people who are not entrepreneurs by nature – though they must have a streak of adventurousness about them. And even the most talented entrepreneur has to learn the craft, and to keep learning, refining and developing his or her skills.

Another misconception about the entrepreneurial character is that, because you are in a steady job in a big organisation, you are not entrepreneur material. Wrong again. Many entrepreneurs come from corporates – they've learned the business from the inside, now it's time to take the knowledge out there and make it work in the way they believe it can. And still more people with 'entrepreneur stuff' remain inside large organisations, for a cocktail of reasons, including security, 'interesting enough' work and habit.

It is a terrible waste of talent – for you and for your employer – if the organisation chooses not to use this most valuable resource.

The entrepreneurial personality?

Some people say there is no such thing.

Management guru Peter Drucker has argued forcefully that enterprise is a discipline, with rules and techniques like any other. Successful entrepreneurs just follow the rules better. We totally accept there is a craft of entrepreneurship – and intend to teach that craft throughout this book – but we also believe that some people are innately better at it than others. Even Drucker admits that 'all entrepreneurs work hard', which is at least one trait, and he also says 'there are clearly people who are more talented innovators than others'. Talent surely implies inbuilt character traits.

The founders of Coffee Republic, Sahar and Bobby Hashemi, entitled the story of their venture *Anyone Can Do It*. It's an excellent book, bringing to life the roller-coaster adventure of founding a business:

recommended reading for potential intrapreneurs, even if they are planning a totally different type of business. However, we don't think it proves the claim of its title. Rather the opposite: the brother-and-sister team emerge as strong characters, who drove their business to success via classic entrepreneur traits such as vision, determination and a capacity for hard work.

We meet many successful entrepreneurs, and they usually fit our profile. A few don't. Rather more think they don't, but anyone who looks at them objectively will tell them that actually they do. Most of them do, and are perceptive enough to admit the fact. They should, after all, be very proud of who they are!

There is one sense in which we agree that 'anyone can do it'. You don't have to come from a particular class, race, gender or background to be an entrepreneur. If you have the 'right stuff', then wherever you start from, you can master the craft. So let's say anyone (with enough of the right character traits) can do it (provided they master the craft).

This is also true within organisations. Intrapreneurs can, and do, come from all levels. This fact may be an embarrassment for some senior managers, but it is a truth that must be faced and embraced.

Beermat.biz

So – are *you* an entrepreneur?

Most of us try and make as much sense of the world as we can –
hard enough sometimes. Entrepreneurs look beyond how
things are, to how they might be *different*. Taking the widest
definition of entrepreneur, we can include social
revolutionaries and artists, both of whom have powerful,
idiosyncratic *visions* – but we are sticking to organisational
enterprise here. More in the next chapter on how this vision
works.

They then go on to put their plan into *action*. Entrepreneurs
aren't just visionaries: they make things happen.

A key entrepreneur trait is *determination* – or stubbornness, if
you prefer. Entrepreneurs will not take no for an answer!

There are many stories about entrepreneurs sticking to their
guns when all around them are saying they are fools (peek
ahead, to pages 164–166). Our personal favourite is about Tim
Smit, the founder of the Eden Project. For those of you who
don't know this remarkable place, it is an ecological tourist
attraction built in old kaolin pits in Cornwall. These pits had
been blots on the landscape for decades, but nobody had done
anything with them, as they used to flood every winter. When
Tim outlined his vision, he was told it was unrealisable because
of this flooding, so he found an expert to keep them dry. But
the expert agreed with the sceptics: sorry, Mr Smit, come
October your project will be underwater.

Entrepreneurs aren't just visionaries: they make things **happen**.

In true entrepreneur fashion, Tim sought out more experts, all of whom told him the same story. Except one, who reckoned he could sort the problem. And who did sort it. The Eden Project is now the third-biggest tourist attraction in England.

Ambition is another crucial entrepreneur trait. Not to make money, but to change things. And, usually, to get a great deal of credit for having done so. OK, they want money too, but this is not as powerful a motive as cynics think.

This point is very important, as one of the arguments against creating a culture of entrepreneurship within a corporation is that the right people won't take it seriously because the entrepreneur's upside of stock maket flotation and accompanying millions are absent. Wrong.

Entrepreneurs are *charismatic*. They attract followers; they get these people to jump through hoops. Business is ultimately a team game: if you cannot inspire and motivate people, you will not turn your idea into a working commercial entity.

They *network well*, using their charisma to create alliances and acquaintanceships, and to make sure that the world is aware of them and where they are headed.

Note that these two last points do not automatically mean that entrepreneurs have great home lives or even many close friends – some do, some don't. Charisma and networking are essentially public, not private, skills.

Entrepreneurs are *positive*. Their optimism is often delightfully irrational, but it needs to be. Almost by definition, the best new ideas seem crazy given the existing state of affairs. Only once things begin changing do they suddenly appear initially to make some kind of sense, then a lot of sense, then to be blindingly obvious. Great ideas are like great tunes – they sound 'easy' in retrospect, but try writing a Mozart aria or a McCartney love-song. During their early life, entrepreneurial ideas need a huge amount of optimism to keep them going. Fortunately, entrepreneurs have this to hand.

Entrepreneurs are often in a great *hurry*. They want things done yesterday. They are not always very tolerant of people who prefer to move more slowly.

Along with this, they are *hard workers*. This may seem obvious, but it's a key difference between people who sound like entrepreneurs – have lots of great ideas, and can attract followers – and people who actually end up creating successful businesses.

So there we have it: visionary, determined, ambitious, charismatic, well connected, positive, in a hurry, hard-working.

Does that sound like you?

Great. Keep reading, please.

There is also a bad side to entrepreneurs, which doesn't get mentioned in the literature on the subject nearly as often as it should.

Entrepreneurs can be appallingly *unfocused*, forever coming up with new ideas. The best ones retain the overall vision – but can't resist tinkering with the way that vision will be expressed in practice. Worse, many of them lose interest once the idea is up and running.

visionary, determined, ambitious, charismatic, well connected, positive, in a hurry, hard-working.

Does that sound like you?

Entrepreneurs can be *arrogant* and *manipulative* – that stubbornness and that charisma have their downside.

They are often *not team players*. The successful ones form teams around them, but they remain the boss. They rarely consider their team as equals – which can be a major problem. We said in *The Beermat Entrepreneur* that entrepreneurs must give their founding team most of the equity, and it was the most unpopular thing we wrote. We met one entrepreneur in the United States who told us proudly that she had read the book and was now sharing the equity in her business with her first cornerstone. Later we found out that the split was 99:1.

So there we have it: the Entrepreneurial Personality. Why are entrepreneurs like this, both good and bad? Our view is that they have to be. If they lacked that vision, that stubbornness, that ability to charm, that optimism, that streak of selfishness, they would not be able to turn ideas into businesses. There are just too damn many obstacles.

Note that we do not include 'addiction to risk' in our list. In some academic literature, this is cited as the touchstone for an entrepreneur. We do not agree: entrepreneurs are not gamblers. Some certainly like risk, and none of them cowers before it, but the best entrepreneurs work hard to minimise the risk once they have chosen their path. What is true is that entrepreneurs choose to work in an environment with stratospherically high levels of *uncertainty* – levels that would leave many corporate managers reeling with vertigo. In the 'jungle' of those emerging markets where entrepreneurs congregate, Goldman's Law applies.

'Nobody knows anything.'

The quote comes from Hollywood producer William Goldman, in answer to a question about how top producers spotted whether scripts, or even finished films, were going to be box-office successes.

Almost all that is good, and bad, about entrepreneurs relates back to this law, and the sort of people they need to be to live with it.

The *Beermat* model of how enterprise – and intraprise – works also arises from this law, and the necessity it imposes on business innovators to test ideas *quickly, cheaply and with the minimum of fuss*. Remember those three criteria, for they are of immense importance.

So where does this leave internal, corporate entrepreneurs – the 'intrapreneurs'?

Our view is that they will share these traits, though to a less extreme degree. Corporate life will have 'knocked a few edges' off the worst traits – for example, the inability to work as part of a team. Corporate life may possibly have blunted the better traits a little, too.

As a result of this, they will probably be regarded as 'a bit of a maverick' – but they will have earned the respect of people they work with. They will also be known in disparate parts of the business, thanks to that entrepreneur love of networking. A few sticklers for protocol, whom they will probably have offended at some time, will probably dislike them. HR may well have reviews bemoaning their 'lack of focus'.

At the same time, they will be loyal company people. They would have left, otherwise. This loyalty is no doubt tempered with pragmatism – the company offers (relative) financial security. But isn't this true of most workplace loyalties? The point is that the intrapreneur wants to do stuff for him- or herself and for the company.

This loyalty is probably the biggest single difference between intrapreneurs and entrepreneurs out there, 'in the wild' (the latter being loyal, above all other calls, to themselves). It is also one of the most misunderstood aspects of the innovation process. Strict company loyalists see anyone with entrepreneurial leanings as unreliable, and possibly also cowardly: 'They'd leave and start their own business, but they haven't the guts, so they stay here, take the company's money and play at being entrepreneurs.' (We've heard this said.) This criticism is grossly unfair – and reveals the speaker to be a dangerous but ultimately slayable 'dragon', of whom more in Chapter Five.

Remember that entrepreneurs are not primarily in it for the money. They want to make a difference. They also want to be recognised as people who make a difference. Intrapreneurs are exactly the same.

The point is that the **intrapreneur** wants to do stuff **for** him- or herself and **for** the company.

Spotting the entrepreneurs within the organisation

Hopefully, those reading this book will be saying, 'That's me!'

Great. This book is here to give you both the inspiration and the practical tools to make your dreams a reality. And to save your organisation, while we're about it.

For the CEO and the HR team: you need these people. How do you spot them?

The best way is via workshops. Simple 'business games' often reveal natural entrepreneurs in unexpected places. Our own Intrapreneurship Workshops (see pages 114–116) are attended by senior managers, who should have their eyes open for raw talent. Who's coming up with the best ideas? Who latches on to the best ideas? Who makes the effort to follow the ideas through, suggesting people who might help with the project, and (most important of all) actually gets hold of and motivates these people? Who chases up management about their promise to implement the ideas? Who rolls up their sleeves and gets a problem sorted when someone goes into 'yes, but...' mode?

Another way of discovering corporate entrepreneurs is to get some long-standing company people into a group, talk them though the intrapreneuring process, then ask them who they think is suitable for this. Ask them for:

★ a person

★ a reason

★ a project they'd like to see this person fulfilling.

A 'potting-shed audit' can help. Find out how many people in the company are working on tiny, personal projects related to work – not dishonest attempts to leverage company assets for private gain, but simple experiments motivated by pure curiosity and interest in the business's technology. Manufacturing businesses will be amazed by the number of employees who are beavering away in their spare time, creating bizarre, imaginative and sometimes even functional gizmos.

These 'potting-shed engineers' may not have all it takes to be intrapreneurs – remember the difference between entrepreneurs and inventors – but they can still have a key role in an intrapreneurial *team*, and teams lie at the heart of intrapreneurial success, just as they do for entrepreneurs. More on this later.

There are also personality tests that show up entrepreneurial traits – see the box on the next page.

Or simply use the world's best psychological selection tool: your intuition.

Once you have the right people, the next task is to get them working on the right project. Note the order: intrapreneurs first, then ideas. In theory, idea selection should come first, but in practice innovation is fundamentally about people, without whom ideas just remain ideas.

Arthur Rock, the great venture capitalist (in the days when venture capitalists were great), once said, 'An idea is simply an excuse for getting a team together to make something happen.'

innovation
is fundamentally about **people**,
without whom
ideas just remain **ideas**.

Testing for intrapreneurs

We weren't particularly complimentary about psychological profiling in *The Beermat Entrepreneur*, because it is of limited use for entrepreneurs. You know yourself if you are an entrepreneur, and when it comes to hiring people, tests are more expensive and less reliable than intuition.

However, in a big company tests can help a large, formal recruitment process. They can also show up employees who have the right stuff, but who for various reasons have been hiding it – many of us don't 'bring our whole selves to work' (if more CEOs read this book and act on it, hopefully many more employees will).

We suggest using the Myers-Briggs Type Indicator, as this is the most commonly used profiling system and thus the best road-tested; also because it was itself a Beermat product. In the 1930s psychological profiling was unreliable. Isabel Myers and Katharine Briggs were amateur, but diligent, students of psychology who set about improving this, creating a new profiling tool based on Jung's theories of personality. As they weren't academics (and no doubt, in those days, also because they were female) their work was not taken seriously by the 'experts'. Luckily, in true Beermat fashion, they had a mentor, Edward Hay, head of HR at a major bank, who encouraged them to work on their product and gave them opportunities to use it. The rest is history.

▶▶

The Myers-Briggs test looks at four key differences between people:

★ where we draw energy from (the world out there, or our inner world)

★ where we seek information (the immediate and tangible, or the theoretical and intuitive)

★ how we assess information (logic or feeling)

★ whether we like structure or freedom.

Given that different sorts of people can choose any option in each of the four categories, this creates 16 possible character 'types'. These types turn out to be very different, and to be reasonably equally divided across the population.

What results should you be looking for? In our model, entrepreneurs belong to a type called ENTP (no, the type names are not hugely evocative) – that is, they are extrovert, big-picture, tough-minded and rebellious, disliking structure. We would also recommend looking at anyone who is P (rebellious) and two out of E, N and T. The INTP types ('I' means introvert) often make good high-tech innovators – our concern would be about their ability to retain and motivate a team. People of type ESTP ('S' people prefer detail to big pictures) often drive through low-level innovations – very useful team members, but do they have the breadth of vision to create innovations that will grow to become substantial businesses? People of type ENFP ('F' people are

▶▶

more tender-minded and people-focused) make great 'social entrepreneurs'.

Sales people, incidentally, tend to be ESFJ – extrovert (of course!), down-to-earth, emotional, but liking a bit of structure.

Myers-Briggs (and other psychological) tests are best administered by a professional, though there are DIY versions around. Get them done properly – it's worth it.

Remember that the point of these tests is not to dissuade people from being entrepreneurs, but to spot people with hidden entrepreneurial potential. Used in this way, they can help unearth valuable hidden treasure. This potential has, of course, then to prove itself in reality.

Beermat.biz

We'll conclude this chapter with one final – and hugely important – point. Earlier on we asked if you fitted the entrepreneur profile. Since then, the text has assumed that you did (enough anyway). But supposing you did not – but are still attracted to the idea of intraprise?

Intrapreneurs
need **teams**.

The good news is that there is still plenty of opportunity. Those visionary, determined, ambitious, charismatic, positive, stubborn, arrogant, unfocused intrapreneurs need teams.

These teams are not composed of other intrapreneurs, but of people who combine entrepreneurial flair with reliability and skill (or, in other cases, simple enthusiasm). And in a truly intrapreneurial company, *everyone's* entrepreneurial leanings – we all have some – can and should be leveraged to the full.

The issue of intrapreneurial teams and how to build them is covered in Chapter Three: right now, the intrapreneur needs to get his or her teeth into an idea.

Chapter Two: **The Right Project**

Entrepreneurs, like writers, are often asked, 'Where do you get your ideas from?' Like writers, their answer is often, 'I don't know.'

However, the entrepreneurial vision can be broken down into steps. It begins with a problem. The entrepreneur asks the Magic Question: 'Where's the pain?'

For example:

★ A salesperson is perpetually being told by customers that they need an X, but there aren't any on the market at the moment.

★ A technician gets increasingly frustrated by a bottleneck.

★ A marketeer becomes convinced that a segment of the market is being poorly served by existing business.

★ An accountant sees costs mounting up in an area of business activity.

★ A consumer wants products that are better-quality, more reliable, cheaper, easier to buy and/or use, or that come with proper service…

'Where's the **pain?**'

People often say in response to the above that a lot of successful enterprise is surely about creating pleasure, not removing pain. In our view this comes later. Once your business is up and running, yes, of course you must delight your customer by delivering brilliantly. When seeking initial inspiration, however, looking for real *needs* is a necessary discipline, to keep you clear of the pitfall tumbled into by too many bright but unsuccessful ideas, that of being 'a solution in search of a problem'. Even in consumer markets, a feeling of 'Grr, I'd love an X right now, but there aren't any available!' is the best place to start.

The next step is to envisage a way of *solving* that pain. Entrepreneurs may not do this on their own – as we say below, they are great networkers, and they may well need information about technology and markets (or whatever) to turn their vision into reality. They will find this information.

The solution often, but not always, lies in some new technology or process: good entrepreneurs have an 'eagle eye for change'. As Peter Drucker points out in the classic essay, 'change' includes surprises: unexpected successes or failures out there (why? – the answers are often revealing).

Thirdly, entrepreneurs work out how their solution will work *as a business* – in other words, how it will make money. This third step represents the difference between entrepreneurs and pure inventors. Pure inventors imagine and build things; entrepreneurs imagine and build businesses.

If you are not sure of where to find 'pain', here are some tips and tricks to set you looking in the right places.

Look at social trends. The entrepreneur's eagle eye for change doesn't just apply to technology. Many great businesses emerge from social change: new legislation, changes in public taste, demographics, the social consequences of new technology.

The entrepreneurial vision

1. *Where's the pain?* The Magic Question.

- ★ customer complaints
- ★ technology bottlenecks
- ★ poorly served markets
- ★ crippling costs
- ★ frustrated consumers

2. *How can we solve it?* Envisage a solution, possibly using new processes or technologies.

3. *How can we do this profitably?* Embed the solution in a workable business model.

Beermat.biz

What pain is being caused by these changes, for whom, and how can you help?

Pure **inventors** imagine and build **things**; **entrepreneurs** imagine and build **businesses**.

Better, nicer, easier or cheaper. An old piece of entrepreneurial wisdom is that to succeed you must be 10 per cent better, nicer, easier or cheaper than the competition. Can you take an existing company offer and improve it that much in one of those directions? (See the section on the 'advantage timeline' on page 38 – if you can't decide which direction.)

Trade radically up or down. 10 per cent is a good start – but many great businesses succeed by adding an extra 0 to this figure, and creating a totally new market. The two obvious ways of doing this are to trade radically up or radically down.

Trading radically up is more unusual (business customers have too close an eye on costs), but can work, especially in consumer markets. Take a range of slightly mundane products and produce something outrageously luxurious, priced way, way above what people are paying at the moment. Guess what? A market may be there, waiting. This is proving particularly successful in America. Pleasant Rowland was a 'frustrated consumer' who wanted a high-quality doll to give to a niece. So she designed a range, with expressive faces and accurate historical costumes, which went on the market for six times the cost of Barbie; 15 years later she sold her upmarket doll company for $700 million.

At the other end of the scale, trade down: not by producing shoddy goods, but by creating a 'disruptive market' by stripping costs out of a formerly frilly, feature-obsessed area of activity and seeing what happens. The best contemporary example is the airline business. The keys to the budget airlines' success are partially a new technology – ticket purchase over the internet – but most of all a *culture of low cost.* This culture is worth examining. Both easyJet and Ryanair were founded by entrepreneurs with a passion for slashing costs, and retain this mindset. All aspects of operations, from airport landing fees to the number of check-out desks, are re-examined endlessly with this end in view. Cost is viewed in the widest sense, so it includes time. There are no dinners on budget airlines, not because they are expensive in themselves, but because loading dinners and clearing them up take up too much aeroplane turnaround time.

Here's a thought for the CEO: imagine a business with a similar attitude to enterprise, which Stelios or Michael O'Leary has to cost... Look at *every* aspect of what you do, and ask, 'Can we let the imagination of our people loose on this?'

The point of the 'disruptive', trading-down-radically approach is that it opens a whole new market to the product. Below, we discuss the ultimate extension of this.

The world's biggest market

In our busy, First World life it's easy to lose sight of the fact that the majority of our fellow human beings – four billion, according to management gurus C.K. Prahalad and Allen Hammond – are still poor. But are they thus beyond the scope of imaginative business? No, say those two authors. The problem is not their poverty, but the perception in unimaginative corporations that these people are 'not worth serving'.

But they are worth serving, and they represent an enormous opportunity to create vibrant businesses and at the same time remove the disgraceful scourge of poverty in our rich, 21st-century world.

The key, Prahalad and Hammond argue, is to create disruptive business models that suit the poorest ▶▶

consumer. Cost must, of course, be stripped out everywhere, and new ways of distribution be considered (many very poor communities don't even have shops, for example). The key is, of course, to see things from the consumers' perspective. Where's their pain? How might they get hold of what they need to solve that?

An example: middle-class consumers save by buying in bulk. Very poor people can't afford to tie capital up like this: they want to buy stuff that we take for granted, like shampoo, sweets or use of a mobile phone, on a 'shot-by-shot' basis. (Products sold this way have been a huge success in rural India.)

Financial institutions have a key role to play in this, not by throwing money at corrupt governments, but by creating business models for extending credit at fair levels to the very poor. At the moment the very poor only have access to grossly overpriced credit – Prahalad quotes a figure of 600 per cent annual interest as 'very common'.

A fantasy? Many of the greatest businesses were founded on the principle of taking a luxury and finding a way of making it available to the ordinary European or American. It's time to do this for the world.

Beermat.biz

Rembrandts in the attic. We've shamelessly borrowed this term from the book by Kevin Rivette and David Kline, because we like it so much. The Rembrandts in question are patents.

Most mature companies don't so much have an attic full of Rembrandts as rooms stuffed with them. Rivette and Kline go through all sorts of ways of leveraging underused Intellectual Property (IP) for strategic battles with rivals – but for the purposes of this book, the dormant patents are there to be revisited and revitalised by intrapreneurs.

Where we disagree with Rivette and Kline is that they suggest a prior audit of patents, with a three-way split, into:

★ patents clustered around the core competencies of the business

★ non-core, but potentially valuable ones

★ non-core, and you can't see much value for them in today's world.

We prefer a more open approach. There will, of course, be some core patents that the company doesn't want to let out of the building: Coke is probably well advised not to let too many intrapreneurs loose on its drink formula. So there should be a screening for 'security risk' first. Once this is done – get intrapreneurial with whatever is left.

IP is notoriously hard to value: whatever 'experts' may say, it has very little value sitting on a shelf (yes, it might have some strategic 'blocking' value, but this is hard to assess). It only really comes into its own as a source of revenue when a team gets behind it, finds real 'pain' for it to solve, and attaches a revenue model to it so that the solving does so profitably. As in the rest of the enterprise world, Goldman's Law is at work. You only find out which IP is really valuable once the right team has made it so.

This knowledge is hugely valuable: a recent survey of US universities showed that 90 per cent of their licence income came from 8 per cent of their patents. But nobody knows in advance which ones are going to be the winners.

For the intrapreneur: do you know the Chief Patent Officer in *your* company?

He or she is worth talking to. And for the CEO: how senior is this person? Does he or she sit in a small office at the end of a long corridor, and meet board members once a year at the annual Christmas party?

Intrapreneurs and their bosses take the whole issue of IP very seriously.

do you know
the Chief Patent Officer
in *your* company?

Evangelism. Evangelists – enthusiasts who spread the word about great new products, ideas (or whatever) – are beloved of salespeople out there on the road. But they can also play a huge role in creating new ideas in a company. Especially in a large one.

Internal corporate evangelists are sophisticated: they really understand what they are talking about, and are eager to spread it throughout the company. The best ones ask people if they have 'pain' that the new idea/process/technology might solve. If the listener is imaginative, the answer may well be 'yes'.

In *How Breakthroughs Happen*, Andrew Hargadon cites two examples, from 3M and from Xerox. In 3M, a technology was developed for concentrating the way light comes off a surface. This was disseminated through the company by evangelists, who found people in other departments working on projects as various as road signs, luminous tape, CD-Roms and drag-reducing coatings for aeroplane wings. All these people, after some thought, found that the new technology – or a development of it – solved pain for them. At Xerox, on the other hand, some of the greatest inventions of the 20th century were made at their famous PARC. But not enough was done with them, as nobody enthused sufficiently to the rest of the company.

Evangelists can also take the message of new internal processes to other parts of the company with 'pain'.

The image that comes to mind is of a room full of brilliant people, who every now and then look up from their desks or workbenches and shout out, 'Has anybody got an A that also does B? I need one desperately!' or 'Does anyone need an X? I've just invented one' or 'Has anyone got a Z that costs less than £1? I've a customer here who has a real problem…'

Actually, Thomas Edison's lab at Menlo Park was not too dissimilar to this.

The matrix. We got through the whole of *The Beermat Entrepreneur* without a single matrix, which must be a record for a business book. However, we think the Ansoff matrix is so good, and so relevant here, that we have to put it in. Anyone who knows it already, and the people who emailed thanking us for keeping *Beermat* matrix-free, will hopefully forgive us. Take a deep breath…

The Ansoff matrix

1. Existing products, existing markets

Incremental innovation

Key issue:
How can we do this better/cheaper/ nicer/quicker?

3. New products for existing markets

First-step Beermat intrapreneurship

Key issues:
Are we really doing all we can?
What else do they need?

2. Selling existing products to new markets

Classic first-step intrapreneurship

Key issue:
Who else would benefit from these things/ services?

4. New products for new markets

Adventurous intrapreneurship

Key issue:
Does anybody actually need/want one of these?

The standard reading of the matrix is that there is a 'path of least resistance' through it. You begin with incremental improvements in Quadrant 1, then move to Quadrant 2, finding new markets for existing products, then to Quadrant 3. There you stop. You should avoid 4 if at all possible.

This is no doubt prudent, but many intrapreneurs like to leap straight to 3, and often have their eyes on the forbidden fourth quadrant. And why not? Leaping to Quadrant 3 is a good strategy for intraprise: you have the customers already, so get talking to them about what other 'pain' there is around for them at the moment that you might be able to solve.

And what about the command 'Keep out of Quadrant 4'? This is exactly where entrepreneurs 'out there in the wild' spend their time, beginning as they usually do with a new product and no proven market. Yes, you should enter this quadrant with care – but what does that mean in practice? It means enter with minimal risk, trying out ideas stealthily, cheaply and as quickly as possible. Exactly what skilled entrepreneurs do all the time.

At the same time, remember that a good Quadrant 1 idea for improving service to current customers is worth much more than a sexy-sounding leap into Quadrant 4 that actually has no business logic at all behind it. As we've said, those change-gurus who despise incrementalism are, in our view, wrong. See pages 114–16 for more on how to create excellent Quadrant One innovation and re-enchant your staff in the process.

Nonetheless, the pulse of the true intrapreneur will inevitably quicken, the further you get from base…

Think 'service'. The service mindset lies at the heart of the Beermat business philosophy. We know this message is not new; it's been around since the 1960s, when Theodore Levitt started asking companies, 'What business are you really in?' Yet it is still not heeded as closely as it should be. As a result there is a tremendous opportunity for intrapreneurs in many organisations.

Service is a perfect vehicle for intraprise. The market is already there, so there is no need for expensive research. Get talking to your customers!

GE's nuclear-reactor business is a classic example. They had been building and selling reactors successfully since the mid-1960s, but with the Three Mile Island meltdown in 1979, the market died overnight. The passionate techies in charge of the division insisted that the meltdown was just a temporary hitch: they'd got these great new designs for the next generation of reactors, and orders would come flooding back... Chairman Jack Welch knew differently, and started switching the business to servicing their existing clients (they already had 72 reactors out there, which other people were servicing). Four years later they hadn't sold another reactor, but were making an annual profit in excess of $100 million from their existing customers.

Get talking to your customers!

If you make Xs, you are probably the best people in the world to install them, to service them, if necessary to decommission them and, most important of all, to teach people how to get the best out of them (or, in the case of many products, how to use them at all). Training is the ideal intraprise – desperately needed by the customer, who's often too embarrassed to admit the fact; easy to provide, as you are the experts in the topic. In good times there's often a nice flexible budget to be paid out of, too.

Note that this doesn't just apply to manufacturers. Software cries out for proper service back-up, and often doesn't get it: a huge amount of the stuff is bought, installed, found to be too difficult to operate and sidelined. The companies that flog this deserve the misery that will undoubtedly overcome them once they find themselves getting no repeat business and once their once-unique software becomes a cheap commodity. Had they had the imagination to add consultancy, coaching and training to their sell, they would have made more money *and* would have had friends for life.

A radical option is to provide the products for cost, or even nothing, and charge largely or only for the consultancy. Why not? This can create more revenue; it leads to customers actually getting what they need. It can also teach you a lot about their business, including a whole raft of other needs they didn't mention at the sales meeting (but which, amazingly, you have exactly the solution for − 'In fact, while our people are here fixing your widgets, why don't we do a temporary grommet fix for you now, and we'll get the proper replacements over first thing tomorrow morning…').

Another advantage of thinking 'service' is cost. Cost is a huge issue to start-ups 'out there', and always has been, apart from during the dot-com boom (and no doubt for railway start-ups in the 1840s, South Sea investors in 1720, and developers of black tulips in the 1630s). Intraprises should treat cost in exactly the same, cautious way. To make new things is expensive. Initially, of course, you blag resources left, right and centre (more on this later), but there soon comes a time when some kind of formal production system has to be set up, at which point a sudden 'lump' of funding usually becomes necessary. Services, on the other hand, have virtually zero start-up costs, and can be grown in a linear fashion.

As we said, many readers may object that this is old hat. 'We do services already.' Really? With 100 per cent customer satisfaction? Using all the latest technology? Our bet is that if the imaginations of the right, intrapreneurial people were let loose on the way you do services, a whole new range of Quadrant 3 products would emerge.

If you run/own a pure, or nearly pure, services company already, then you will be aware of the need for perpetual innovation. 'We have to make constant changes,' says Rupert Sebag-Montefiore, MD of upmarket property consultants F.P.D. Savills. 'Anyone who stops doing this is soon left behind by the market.' Thinking 'service' is not a one-off change, but a commitment to an unending process.

The 'advantage timeline'. Returning to the old adage that we mentioned earlier in this chapter: to break into a market you have to be 10 per cent better, nicer, easier, or cheaper than the existing competition... As an approximate rule, there is an order for delivering these benefits, depending on how mature the market is. This roughly fits in with the product cycle model of 'early adopters' (who'll buy anything that does the job), 'early majority' (a much bigger and less technology-focused market, who won't buy without reliability) and 'late majority' (who assume reliability and will only buy from you if you make it easy or nice for them to do so).

Note that the 'radical trading down' discussed earlier in this chapter is effectively the creation of a new market, so it starts back at the beginning of the timeline. It is 'step innovation', creating a whole new class of product, not trying to shift the same stuff as a load of other people – the hell of price wars in mature markets.

Thinking 'service' is not a one-off change, but a commitment to an unending process.

The advantage timeline

Early adopter phase. When a market is *new*, anything that does the job will sell.

Early majority phase. The market gets a little *more sophisticated*; competition switches to quality:

★ reliability

★ precise fit to task

★ beauty, craftsmanship (for consumer goods).

Late majority phase. Once *quality becomes standard*, customers seek convenience and niceness:

★ size

★ easy to buy; easy to use

★ friendly service.

Maturity. Once convenience and niceness are standard, then the *price wars* begin.

Beermat.biz

Note also that you can add service and training at any point on the timeline.

Early adopter service will be all about hand-holding, sorting problems when the gizmos break down (again!), and reminding the customer how much pain they solve (when they work, which is after all most of the time…). Training is for the experts.

Early majority service is about regular maintenance and ensuring continuity of benefit in the rare event of one of the gizmos failing. Training is now for everyone who goes near the gizmo.

For the late majority, service is about coming in with a smile, just to check everything is OK. Training could be about advanced gizmo use for the techies, or fun with gizmos for everyone else.

By selecting the battleground on which you wish to fight, you can enter a market anywhere on the timeline – except when the issue has become price, where you'd be mad to do so, unless you have real step innovation and a 'radical trade-down' strategy.

The point of including these matrices and timelines is to get ideas flowing. In the end, the idea that works will not be the one that rolls most easily off any formal idea creation model. It'll be the one that, by a process more like falling in love than coming to a rational business decision, takes root in your mind, then in your guts, then in your soul – so you end up furious if you can't do it.

You can't do it, however, not even in the most intrapreneurially minded company. Not on your own.

Chapter Three: The Right Team

Solo entrepreneurs nearly always fail.

This doesn't mean that people can't become 'sole traders' and make a living, but it does mean that entrepreneurs who dream of creating great businesses all by themselves (so that they can have all the credit and all the fame) will fail. Great businesses are built by teams – headed and driven by an entrepreneur, of course.

Sadly, we meet an awful lot of solo entrepreneurs, and spend a lot of time listening to them bemoan their lot. We tell them to form teams, but they always come up with splendid reasons why they can't. It's a bit like those people who decide to walk to the North Pole unaided. Unlike polar explorers, who usually get on the news and get rescued, these lone entrepreneurs plod off unnoticed into the snowstorm. If they are lucky, they don't give up the day job, and when the idea fails they can put it down to experience.

Great businesses are built by teams

This truth about entrepreneurship is actually rather good news for the corporation, which, remember, is not just looking out for ideas, but for *ways of testing ideas quickly, cheaply and with the minimum of fuss.* If an intrapreneur 'falls in love' with the idea: great start. If that person cannot build a team around that idea, then – as in the wild – the idea has no real chance of survival, and has thus been subjected to a powerful test, at zero cost to the employer.

Taking a passionate intrapreneur plus an idea, then putting them through a formal selection process involving committees, Venture Boards and so on, then seconding people to them with orders to go and fix it, is wasteful and unnecessary. Much better to see if they can attract and retain a team.

The team-building process often begins with…

The foil

The first team member that the successful entre- and intrapreneur attracts is often a 'foil', another person with whom they work closely, who complements what they do. Foils are often rather quieter and more reflective than intrapreneurs, but they also often quietly bring a key part of the IP.

As a result of their more cerebral nature, the buy-in by a foil is a clear signal that the idea and the intrapreneur (you can't really separate the two, once they have 'clicked') have got what it takes. Or at least that they've got a fighting chance.

Foils often like to stay in the background. The Virgin empire is often seen as being synonymous with its dashing founder, Sir Richard Branson – and why not? (it's excellent branding). But for many years Branson built up his empire together with a finance cornerstone, Robert Devereux, who was in our view just as important as the talented frontman.

The founding team

Even two people aren't really enough, however. In *The Beermat Entrepreneur* we imagined people sitting in a pub thinking up business ideas. After the idea itself, the first thing they had to write on their beermats (nobody had brought any paper) was a *mentor* for the project. The intrapreneur is even more in need of such a person than the 'wild' entrepreneur. Within the corporation, we refer to such people as sponsors – more on them below.

The new venture will soon need a full complement of *cornerstones*. There is no more important issue for start-ups than the make-up of their founding teams: if a start-up is struggling, it is almost always because there is no balanced business team at its heart. Do not let this happen to your internal enterprise!

Once the founding team has got the business off the ground, new people will join the team. The first 20 or so will be a *Dream Team* of very special people.

To expand on these three essential categories of sponsors, cornerstones and Dream Team…

The sponsor

All entrepreneurs 'out there' should find themselves a mentor: a senior and experienced business person who gets their idea, likes the entrepreneur, and whom the entrepreneur likes. The mentor fulfils two essential roles – offering advice and opening doors.

The internal entrepreneur may think he or she can dispense with this. 'I've been in this company long enough to know my way around. If people at the top get involved, they'll only get in the way, and might take all the credit if things go well…'

Wrong.

It is true that most intrapreneurs will probably have a better understanding of general business matters than many entrepreneurs 'in the wild' (especially than those very young entrepreneurs you read about, who seem to start straight from the cradle selling rattles to their friends). They are probably also better at the personal stuff than their external counterparts.

But this is balanced out by the context in which the internal entrepreneur has to work – the company. A big company is a huge maze of people and processes, often divided into numerous divisional and geographical areas. Nobody can understand all of these, but the chances are that a more senior person will have a better overview.

More important still, this maze isn't just a passive place. It is forever changing – and it's hostile. There are people out there who will take an active dislike to your project and try and destroy it, for a range of motives we discuss later: this maze is full of dragons, and negotiating it requires protection, which you can only get from someone senior within the organisation.

Finding a mentor can be a major headache for entrepreneurs. It's often the first serious test of themselves and their idea. For internal entrepreneurs it should be easier – depending, of course, on the culture of the company.

You know your company and its culture. Are there formal sponsoring programmes in place (also known as mentoring or championing programmes)? If so, that's a great start. But it is still just a start, as you have to get into the programme and emerge with the right sponsor. To remind you of what makes that person 'right' …

They like you. Remember, you are undoubtedly going to be asking this person to stick their neck out for you. They are unlikely to do this if there is not a strong personal rapport between you. Consider why people sponsor in the first place. If there is a strong mentoring culture in the company, it may be because they perceive that's 'the thing to do'. More likely, they're doing it because they want others to benefit from their knowledge. Often the best sponsors are people near the top of the organisation, who: a) know they won't get quite to the top, but b) know they still have a hell of a lot to offer.

The key point is that people sponsor because they enjoy doing it. And a big part of that pleasure is personal chemistry.

Can you get sponsors to like you? We think not. You just have to be yourself. If conscious effort goes into 'presenting yourself' to a sponsor, it should be about clearing away falseness. You would not be a proper intrapreneur if you were not passionate about your idea, so let that passion show. In many corporate settings you have to trim enthusiasm to suit an occasion: when talking to your sponsor, you don't have to do this. Admit to your dreams!

Don't be dispirited if your first attempt at finding a sponsor fails. Don't assume that 'everyone up there is like that'. Keep looking.

people **sponsor**
because they
enjoy doing it.

You must like them. If there's someone senior who loves your idea, appears to like you, but whom you take a dislike to – this isn't going to work. You should probably have a long think about why you dislike this person (are you being overprotective of your idea?), but at the end of the day you must go with your intuition.

The personal chemistry between sponsor and intrapreneur is essential. This is where most formal mentoring schemes fail: people are appointed as mentors and 'mentees', and, while they get on well enough, there's no 'click', no chemistry. What usually happens is that, after a couple of meetings, both sides start making excuses not to meet again, usually due to time pressures, and the relationship withers away.

They get your idea. This third aspect of the relationship is clearly important, though the personal stuff is what really matters, especially at first. 'That's a crazy idea, but I like you so much I'll back you far enough down the line to at least give it a basic test' is a fine response.

How do you set about finding a sponsor? As in all business activity, a little research helps. If there are other mavericks in the company (and you are not deadly rivals), ask them who is open to new ideas. Get to know people in HR, who may well know a lot about the top people and their interests. Draw up a 'hit list' of potential sponsors. Know their areas of expertise, their corporate history – essential when you ask them to open doors – and (as far as you can) their temperament. Are they like you? It is our view that opposites repel, not attract. And if there is a formal mentoring system in the company, do use it – unless you have for some reason decided that it doesn't work any longer.

Don't be afraid to take a punt. As an intrapreneur, you'll be doing a lot of this, so start now. Sir Magnus may have a reputation as a bit of a bear, but if you can't help feeling there's actually a teddy inside waiting to leap out and cuddle someone: give it a try. And if you come out of the encounter severely mauled, fine. You'll receive plenty more knocks in your

intrapreneurial career. Learn from this one and move on to the
next candidate.

There's an optimum way to approach potential sponsors.
Contact their PA, by phone or email. Ask for five minutes of
their (the PA's) time face-to-face. They will almost
undoubtedly give you this time – if not, try someone else or a
direct approach to the sponsor.

During your five minutes with the PA, be open. You've got
this great idea and you are looking for their boss to help you
with it. Get the PA enthusiastic about the idea, if possible.
They may say that their boss is busy – meet this objection with
the request that you only want 15 minutes of the boss's time.

Don't overrun your five minutes with the PA, or they will
conclude that you are also going to waste their boss's time.
Make a formal appointment, and stick to it. Be prepared to be
messed around a bit about this, but if the postponements mount
up, push for a firm meeting. You are entitled to this – as a
senior member of the company, the potential sponsor should
have the politeness and integrity to honour a commitment to
talk to you.

Before every meeting, refine your idea (more about this further
on) so that you have a clear vision of the product, the market
and how you will develop it within the company. (These will,
of course, change as the product encounters reality, but
sponsors will understand this.)

When you meet the sponsor, be yourself. You believe
passionately in this idea – share the passion.

Remember, the sponsor wants to enjoy the journey. Make it
fun for them. Have in your mind a couple of quick things they
could do straight away to help you – if there is no mentoring
culture in the company, they may well fancy the idea but not
know exactly what to do. Make it easy for them, as well as fun.

Don't feel 'they'll be too busy to help'. If they want to help, they'll find time. People are never too busy to do things they believe in. It is also the case that many senior people are very good time managers, and will actually be less 'busy' than some of their subordinates, who have less to do, but are a lot less able at managing their workload.

Once the link is established – use it. Arrange to meet regularly: half an hour once a month is a good target. Make those meetings worthwhile. For yourself: have a clear list of things that you need. For the sponsor: keep them informed of what is going on. When you have a production facility up and running, make the sponsor your first visitor. If you have a party to celebrate a big win, make sure they are invited.

Above all, when your sponsor gives you advice, take it. We often meet mentors of entrepreneurs who lament the fact that their 'charges' won't listen. They end up feeling like Cassandra, the prophet in Greek mythology who was cursed to foresee the future perfectly, but to have no one pay the slightest attention to her predictions.

share the passion.

The art of sponsoring

Looking at the process from the other side… The most important thing about sponsoring is that you enjoy it. If you are doing it because you think you should, or because you think some kind of corporate benefit will accrue to you, think twice. You are senior enough not to do this stuff if it doesn't excite you, so don't do it!

If you are in two minds, consider the pleasures of sponsorship. Did you ever have this great idea that never got put into practice because things weren't done like that in the 'old days'? Here's a fresh chance. Or did you once have lots of success with new ideas, but now seem to be forever mired in organisational processes? Time to get back to your roots. Do you want to meet bright new people in the company – future leaders, perhaps? Or have you always wanted to shake things up a bit, but never felt the moment was right?

Once you decide to be open to sponsorship requests, brief your PA to that effect. Part of their job, remember, is to filter people who want to speak to you. Let your filter know that enthusiastic intrapreneurs are on your 'want to see' list.

The best selection tool at your disposal is your instinct – for the person, more than for the idea. Are they truly passionate about the idea, not just doing it because they read this amazing book on Boardroom Entrepreneurship or because the company has let it be known that intrapreneurship is a way up the ladder? Are they disciplined enough to carry it through? Have they got what it takes to build and motivate a team around them? Above all, did you enjoy your 15 minutes with them? Did you find it refreshing and exciting, or a bit of a chore?

You have to be certain, as your protégé will take up increasing amounts of your time and, more important, will ask you for favours. Are you prepared to put yourself on the line for this person and this idea?

No? Deliver a clear, polite refusal. If there is any feedback you can give the applicant, about their attitude or their idea, provide it – in a positive way: the point is to help them get it right next time. If there is anyone you know who might be right for this person, network them.

Yes? Fantastic. This should be a lot of fun, and could make a huge difference to the company.

What will you be doing?

★ *Giving advice*. Personal, business and 'corporate' – the latter probably the most important of all. The corporation is a maze without a ground plan (it may have the appearance of one, but you know how things really work; or at least you know better than most people…).

★ *Asking the right questions*. These are often the simplest questions: 'Where's the pain?' (you should be able to answer that one) or 'Who would buy such a thing?' (the first question that Mike's mentor, Sir Campbell Fraser, asked him when he joined software company RiverSoft) or 'Yes, but why should they buy it from you in particular?' Such questions sound obvious – until you've met as many entrepreneurs as we have, with amazing technology/designs (etc.), who haven't asked them.

★ *Opening doors*. More than just guiding, you will be called upon to use your influence to get people to give your protégé 15 minutes of their time, the use of some currently idle resource or some scarce resource that is essential to the intraprise.

★ *Protecting them*. This is perhaps your most important, and risky, function. The intrapreneur will attract all kinds of opposition and it will be your job to protect them from this. This is where your commitment to the intrapreneur, their team and their idea will be most put to the test.

There is also another thing you will be doing: keeping an eye on the intraprise, to make sure it doesn't 'overstep' its mark. The reality of most internal start-ups is that they don't upset existing customer relationships – actually they deepen them, because the customers like the passion and focus of the new business. But upsets can happen, and you need to be watching for danger signs. More on this in the section on the culture of the intraprise in Chapter Four.

The elements of sponsorship

★ Establish good chemistry

★ Protect the intrapreneur and intraprise at the highest level

★ Show them the way round the corporate maze

★ Ask the right questions

★ Open doors

★ Advise

★ Keep an eye open for 'brand abuse'

Beermat.biz

Like all human relationships, the sponsor/protégé one can go wrong. Even if the procedure and spirit described above are followed – in other words, if there is a real personal relationship alongside clear business goal-setting and monitoring – things can still change. However strong the friendship, there is always an issue of status, and this has a habit of inveigling itself into things. Is the sponsor 'rescuing' the protégé too often? Is the protégé resenting having to ask for favours? Does either suddenly feel the other has some kind of "hidden agenda'? Or feel they are 'using' the other person?

You have to be honest, first with yourself, then with the other person, if niggles start creeping in. Discuss things openly – you have nothing to lose – and, if ways must part, then that's how it has to be. But this should not happen lightly. Becoming a sponsor is a large responsibility, which is why the right sort of people love taking it on.

Cornerstones

Once the intrapreneur has found a sponsor for their idea, their next challenge is to build a team. A Balanced Business Team. (We'd call it a BBT, but we're fed up with acronyms). This is the area where most 'wild' start-ups fail: an unbalanced team accrues (rather than is properly built), then slowly teeters over.

In theory, it should be easier for the internal entrepreneur to build a balanced team, as there are people with the right skills all around you. Many entrepreneurs 'out there' don't know anyone who is good at sales – you should have contacts in the sales department. And what about finance? Again, many entrepreneurs know nobody with skills in this area, and rely on someone coming in from time to time to 'do the books'. Often someone rather docile. This can end in disaster: when things start going wrong financially, the hired hand either says nothing until it's too late or has the courage to speak up and is rewarded by being fired by the entrepreneur.

An adage of Mike's is that 'A tame accountant tells you you've gone broke, a Finance Cornerstone says you'll go broke in three months unless you do something about it.'

The Balanced Business Team was one of the more radical suggestions of *Beermat*. Entrepreneurs tend to believe they can do everything themselves: one of the reasons for the plethora of docile 'book-doer' accountants is because so many entrepreneurs reckon they can 'handle the serious financial stuff themselves'. And as for sales…

We've heard people argue that in an intraprise you have less need for a balanced team. The intrapreneur will be more grounded than their 'wild' counterpart, and there will be people with skills in finance and sales keeping an eye on things, anyway.

We disagree. The aim of intraprise is to create a brilliant new business, nothing less. And to be brilliant, the business needs its own experts, who live, breathe, eat and sleep it. Nothing else will do.

In the Beermat model, we say that the founding team should consist of five people. This is the lowest odd number that allows real room for argument (three too often ends up as two-against-one, while seven is already too diffuse). It also enables the team to cover the main bases of business knowledge, namely:

★ innovation

★ delivery

★ sales

★ finance

while keeping an overall role for the entrepreneur. These people are the cornerstones on which the business is based.

The entrepreneur provides drive and vision; the sponsor provides advice, opportunities and protection; these four specialists – the four cornerstones – provide the solidity. Cornerstones are very special people, because they must combine a thorough professionalism with adventurousness.

They must share the entrepreneur's passion for the new, risky idea *and* be able to keep an objective eye on how the idea is being rolled out.

These **people** are the cornerstones on which the **business** is based.

The technical cornerstones. The mindsets of the two technical cornerstones, innovator and deliverer, are very different: the innovator envisions new ideas, and designs and probably builds the prototype, while the deliverer irons out problems with the prototype and turns it into a mass product, designing the manufacturing process and overseeing it. More fully…

The **innovator** focuses on the 'pain' and on radical new ways of overcoming it. They have to start from the position that current methods aren't good enough, and bring lateral, imaginative thinking to bear on the problem. Resources? Assume they're infinite, and play with what you could do.

Innovators rarely finish things. Leonardo da Vinci was probably the greatest innovator in history: the criticism made of him at the time was that 'he never completes anything'. His great rival Michelangelo actually goaded him into a fight with this accusation. Thomas Edison, our number-two candidate for the greatest innovator ever, solved the problem by surrounding himself with 'deliverer' assistants.

Deliverers have to be more plodding, more perfectionist. They are the realists, painfully and perpetually aware of the actual constraints of cost and other resource shortages. Temperamentally, they are not happy until something is working – not a problem for the innovator, for whom the buzz comes once they have made the conceptual leap and built a model that shows it sort-of working.

Note: one of these cornerstones may be the entrepreneur (almost always the innovator), in which case a cornerstone space is vacant. You can either leave it vacant and run the risk of having a 2:2 split on a range of issues, or find a specialist in some key area of delivery to complement the delivery cornerstone's more general outlook. We call such a person a *bottleneck cornerstone*.

The sales cornerstone. Lack of a good sales cornerstone is the single biggest difficulty we find among start-ups. You should have no problems filling this niche.

Later on we talk about the value of networking to the intrapreneur. As part of this practice, you should have made friends in different parts of the company – including sales. Many of the people you meet *and like* on this trans-company networking will be cornerstone material. That's probably why you liked each other to start off with. So talk to the people you have met and liked in the sales department, and find which ones: a) find the idea irresistible, and b) have half a chance of getting involved.

They may not be the 'top salespeople' in the department. They probably spend too long listening to customers to make the quick, quick, quick sales that sales superstars make. They probably have unusual ideas of who might want the product, which often don't work out.

Sales superstars tend to be very good at selling existing products to pre-qualified customers. Your sales cornerstone is doing something much subtler. However brilliant your idea may seem, it probably isn't quite right. It nearly fulfils customer needs, but not quite. The only way to get it really right is to talk to customers, find out what they need, trial the product with them, amend it according to what goes well and what goes badly, retrial (and so on). In other words, once the product is past the prototype stage, you *negotiate* its future form with your biggest customers. This negotiation is a key job of the sales cornerstone.

If you are attacking Ansoff Quadrants 2 or 4 (see page 34), the sales cornerstone will also have to go out and find new customers. Exciting stuff! But once the new customers are found and are listening, the issue is, as above, negotiation (even in Quadrant 2, they will probably want your 'existing products' reconfigured in some way). Where's their pain? How exactly do they want your X?

This need to negotiate the precise nature of the product is, of course, why the sales cornerstone must be at the heart of the Founding Team. A business dominated by technologists will spend far too long developing the product along lines suggested by the technology – which may lead to overspecification and excessive cost. The real role of the sales cornerstone is to be the perpetual, nagging voice of the customer(s) in any and every decision you make.

The technology trap

Technology is wonderful. Without it, where would the enterprise economy be? Three rousing cheers for technology!

Well, let's make it two, quite rousing cheers. Technology can be a trap, into which many fine business ideas tumble headlong, never to emerge. ▶▶

The problem is focus. Technology-based businesses spend too much time on the technology and not enough time looking at the marketplace. A mentality develops – 'Just wait till we've fixed the X problem' – which puts the rest of the business into paralysis.

A 2002 survey in Cambridge showed that 20 per cent of companies in the area 'completely disregarded building market awareness until the product was ready to be launched'. That was an awful lot of effort spent making things nobody might want.

Even with the most high-tech application, the sales cornerstone should start talking to potential customers at once, finding out exactly what those customers' most pressing issues are. The chances are that these needs will not be quite what the developers of the technology imagined. A debate must follow, in which the sales voice must be as loud as the technological one.

So that's happened, and the developers are now working on a customer-driven agenda rather than one formed by the inherent challenges of the technology. This is good – though maybe slightly duller for the developers. But there's still more you can do.

The customer, remember, has a problem right now. Anything you can do to help will be valued. Even if the software crashes from time to time, it may still provide such a useful service that the customer is grateful for it. So provide them with imperfect product – not (and this is the key) in the spirit ▶▶

of fobbing them off, but in the clearly stated understanding that you are working on improvements. Version 0.9 is on its way, and as special-status early customers, they'll be the first to receive it. Maybe they'll even help you fund its development…

The technology cornerstones will probably dislike this, and so might the entrepreneur. Many entrepreneurs are passionate custodians of 'brand value'. While they are up to a point right to be so, beyond this point they are wrong: waiting for perfection can cause fatal delay – and, incidentally, shows a lack of understanding as to what brands really are (trust earned from customers, not abstractly perfect products).

Perfectionist paralysis seems to be a particular problem for academic spin-offs. We have seen many presentations by such teams, which have been largely along the lines of 'Isn't this technology amazing!', plus a couple of slides at the end suggesting some PLCs that might be interested, or featuring those vague, vast market forecasts beloved of dot-coms. This isn't good enough, and it's really heartbreaking, as the technology *is* amazing, but nobody's going to buy it in its current, user-unfriendly form.

We believe this is also a problem within large companies, where R and D teams are sitting on great IP, but somehow it doesn't get turned into profit. There is a solution! ▶▶

Great technology spin-offs need a proper team around them, not of more technologists but of entrepreneurs and sales and finance cornerstones. Great inventors/ researchers/academics should learn the arts of networking (to meet these people) and teamwork (to ensure fruitful cooperation once they have met). Maybe a little respect all round is needed too: business types stop considering academics as nerds, if techies stop regarding entrepreneurs and salespeople as spivs, and accountants as anal retentives...

The outlook for such teams is stellar. The marriage of great technology with entrepreneurial passion, profound customer awareness and solid financial management is one made in heaven. Why are there not more such marriages on earth?

⬛Beermat.biz

Why a *sales* cornerstone, and not marketing? We find marketing too abstract a discipline for the start-up, even when attacking the 'new customers' quadrants. It comes into its own later, but for now you need the Beermat salesperson's skill at building a rapport with individual people.

In fact, it's a sad truth that marketing people in big companies are often the worst enemies of radical innovation. It takes time for radical products to assert themselves in the marketplace – so when the marketing people do their research, they find no interest, and thus damn the new idea. In doing so, they are not being stupid. Using the criteria they have developed, which usually work well, the new product doesn't cut the mustard. (See Clayton Christensen's excellent *The Innovator's Dilemma* for more on this unfortunate fact of business life.)

In the jungle of enterprise, there is no substitute for irrational conviction. 'I just know there's a market out there, and I'm going to find it, come hell or high water.'

Individual marketeers can, of course, be brilliant intrapreneurs or sponsors.

In the jungle of enterprise, there is no substitute for irrational conviction.

The finance cornerstone. As with the sales cornerstone, this person is best discovered by networking throughout the company. Just as there are some sales people who only want to work on existing products, so there will be some finance people who won't go near an internal enterprise. But there are always more adventurous people who will.

Don't be put off by the stereotype of finance people as dull. Some may be – though for us the epitome of dullness is the bad sales person who drones on and on about their product range – but you should have weeded out the dullards while networking.

More of a problem is the attitude and skill set. Finance in the large corporation:

★ is a team effort, like a big audit

★ uses existing systems

★ views cash management as part of the job, although this is often overridden by powerful lobbies of technologists or by marketing people eager to build the brand through expensive advertising

★ allows a junior or mid-ranking person to have little input into strategy.

In the start-up, things are radically different.

★ You start on your own, with an assistant later as the business grows.

★ Systems are initially cheap and simple – but you can design your own.

★ Cash management is crucial (and you have to be ruthless about it).

★ You have huge input into strategy.

For some people in a mid-ranking finance role, the challenges of an intraprise are very exciting. Note that, 'as in the wild', the finance cornerstone does not have to be full-time from the beginning. As long as they have board voting power, they don't need to be in the office every day.

The outside perspective. There is an interesting debate as to whether cornerstones can be recruited from outside the company. It's certainly easier not to; partly for complex cultural reasons, partly for simple practicality.

It's important that the rest of the business sees the intraprise as part of the corporate effort. That way you can enjoy all the 'intrapreneur advantages' we talk about later, to the max. Later, once the business is a flourishing division, it may be spun off –

but that's way in the future. Right now you need to be, and be seen to be, a corporate baby.

But on the other hand… Outsiders can add perspective. If they are any good, they will bring a new set of contacts as well. And if you are assembling a team who are all past masters of big-company stuff, but dying to have a crack at something new, it might be very wise to have at least one experienced start-up specialist in the founding team. Especially if you are planning to charge into the 'new customers' quadrants of the Ansoff matrix, and the outsider is an expert in that market.

The keys to getting this right are flexibility and delicacy. As a general principle, you should look to hire within. But management ought to be aware of the possible benefits of selective introduction of outsiders. 'Selective' is the magic word!

As part of a general enterprise culture programme, why not do things the other way round, and get the company involved with 'wild' entrepreneurs in a strategic alliance? More on this option later.

The Dream Team

Once you have the Founding Team – intrapreneur plus four cornerstones – in place, you do not want any more 'chiefs'. You need more junior people, but not just any kind of gopher. We call these individuals 'Dream Team' members, because the spirit of start-up is very like that of a sports team. They are extremely important.

'Dream Teamers' are young (at heart), energetic, hard-working, excited about the business and, above all, 'doers'. The world does seem to divide into people who get things done, and people who find excuses for not doing things – Dream Teamers are firmly in the former category.

Finding these people should be easy: there should be plenty of them in the company. If there aren't, you're in more trouble than you thought.

Managing them is also easy, if you do it right. The key is to remember that these sort of people want to enjoy their work. They want to make a difference, to find self-respect in their work, and to be respected by their peers for doing it.

They also want to belong, hence the sports–team analogy. The best sports teams know each other well: they can predict each other's moves, ideas and moods. They like and trust one another. 'All for one and one for all', is the ideal motto for the Dream Team. They have a huge loyalty to the group, often feeling 'It's us against the world!' ('And we're going to win!')

The growing new business unit, of which the Dream Team is part, is like a tribe, with you, as intrapreneur, as the chief. But you are more than this, even: you are also the creator of the all-important culture of the team – of which more in the next chapter.

'All for **one** and **one** for all',

Team spirit

Psychological investigation shows that a range of temperaments is needed for teams to work at their best. The problem with much of this work is that it was done in large companies. The classic model of Dr Meredith Belbin has nine different character types making up the perfect team – but the team that will drive your start-up intraprise comprises only five people.

Our solution is to simplify. There seem to be three fundamental psychological types needed in the small team:

★ **Drivers** are entrepreneurs/innovators, always buzzing with ideas, charismatic and energetic. Sales cornerstones are Drivers, too – 'Resource Investigators' in Belbin terminology.

★ **Deliverers** are the people who actually get the work done – in the Beermat team, the delivery cornerstone (obviously) and most of the Dream Team.

★ **Diplomats** negotiate between the two (and between Drivers who start arguing with one another, and between any perfectionist Deliverers). They also do what Belbin calls 'monitoring and evaluating' – in other words, standing back and asking the difficult questions.

The start-up will probably begin with Drivers. There will be a temptation to get even more

Drivers on board, but actually what is needed almost at once is Deliverers. The Drivers may consider these people a little beneath them, but they should not. Do you want to have a business or just to sit around enthusing about having a business? The first Diplomat can be your sponsor, though it is advisable to have one of the five founders who fits this role. Finance, probably.

A balanced business team, where all the key *functions* are represented, is essential to the start-up. But the team needs to be balanced *temperamentally*, too.

⟨Beermat.biz

Chapter Four: **The Right Style**

The new business must – and will – have a nature and style all of its own. A *culture*. Some people get put off by this word: don't be. It doesn't have to be the sort of thing Melvyn Bragg would make a TV programme about. Any and every group of people that co-exists for any length of time has a culture, whether it chooses to or not.

What makes a culture?

Values. It is because values are so important that we say 'hire on intuition, not paper qualifications'. Sharing a culture is about agreeing what matters and what is trivial, what is good and what is bad.

Mythology. Traditional peoples have wonderful epic mythologies about the creation of the world, the miracle of birth, the nature of men and women (and so on). The mythology of your business will be rather less ambitious, but it is still important. How did the company begin? What were its darkest moments, and how did you get out of them? What was your biggest lucky break? Just as tribal myths are peopled with larger-than-life characters, so the company mythology will feature tales of eccentric early employees – probably rather exaggerated, but true to the essence of those people. These won't all be tales of heroic endeavour. Remember the night when Jim got so drunk he ended up in the bus station in Tooting? The time Julie pressed the wrong button on her handset and started telling the chief purchaser of Megacorp about her encounter with the waiter in Tenerife?

Mythology supports values by embedding them in stories, and by giving those stories value. Even the two rather foolish examples given above do this, showing that the new business values high spirits and zest for life.

Note that the big company has a mythology, too, but probably doesn't use it.

The real, entrepreneurial 'creation story' vanishes, and the boardroom fills up with pictures of stern-looking chairmen behind walnut desks or toting Purdeys round country estates.

The **big** company has a **mythology**, too, but **probably** doesn't use it.

Rituals. We lack these in our society, and we think this is a loss. Marriages and funerals are obvious survivals, but otherwise we only participate vicariously in 'national' events such as Live Aid or mourning Princess Diana's death. Rituals are hugely important, for reminding people of the culture's values and mythology and of their shared membership of the group. The original meaning of the word 'religion' was 'binding together again', which is exactly what ritual does.

Mike's company, The Instruction Set, had a very strong culture. Values were straightforwardness, shrewdness, tolerance, hard work, fun, and a sense of humour. The mythology began before the company did – three of the five founders were involved in a student revue that went up to Edinburgh and ran successfully at the Fringe. The revue was down-to-earth (straightforwardness, humour); it was successful because the team did a deal with a prime venue (shrewdness); the Edinburgh Fringe is not a place for the narrow-minded (tolerance); and the whole thing was damned hard work and great fun.

Instruction Set values were reasserted by 'rituals' of weekly pub nights. These were good bonding sessions, but also provided opportunities to spot cliques forming and dissent – which was then dealt with in a straightforward way by sitting the dissenters down and talking through issues. There were also monthly company awards. The awards varied from the serious ('Unsung Hero') to the humorous ('Pranny of the Month'). Mike won the latter once for having the spoiler of his company car chewed by baboons on a visit to a safari park.

Values also, of course, rule out certain behaviour. In a recent 'reality TV' show the participants made a concentrated effort to create a culture. Bitching was frowned on; they regularly had a group huddle; they even adopted the Dream Team motto 'All for one and one for all', and an overall mission – they were going to enjoy the experience, and anything that threatened this mission was to be examined and sorted. (Sadly, this version of the show was branded dull by the critics, and the producers have since spiced it up to feature more temperamental individuals: you have to be selective in taking cultural cues from popular TV!)

By definition, big companies cannot have the warm, tribal culture of small ones, where everyone knows everyone else. Japanese companies with their company song in the morning have a go at this, but it's not the same. Our experience is that once a group has more than about 25 people, it is too big for a really close culture. But you can still have something fun and 'involving' with up to about 150 people, at which point you really do have a large, formal organisation. We talk about this more in Chapter Eight.

The challenge for the intrapreneur, of course, is that you are moving out of a big-company culture and setting up a small business, which will have a totally different culture. But what a great challenge! You can really set the agenda for a group of people, not just in business terms, but in personal and ethical ones. In other words, you can be a real leader. This has interesting implications for the company, which we shall develop in Chapter Seven.

Some leadership tips…

First, *select the right people*. Your cornerstones should be people you trust totally, ideally because you have known them for a while. The difficulties arise when you come to selecting the Dream Team. Select on character, not on apparent merit. Key virtues are enthusiasm, optimism and honesty.

Anyone who looks as if they might have a 'hidden agenda' (for example, of proving they are better than other people in some way – cleverer, cooler, smarter, even nicer) should not be taken on.

As part of your networking, you should have contacts in HR who will be able to suggest cornerstones and Dream Teamers – but use your own personal contacts first.

Enthusiasm,
optimism
and honesty.

Having selected well, *set out dos and don'ts from the start*. And mean it. Reward teamwork, 'mucking in', imagination, extra effort and, most important of all, anyone who encourages or helps a colleague in difficulty. Anyone who starts engaging in point-scoring, one-upmanship or 'mind games' – the expression of the hidden agendas mentioned above – should be given a warning, then dismissed.

You should *have a vision* of what the new company means. What it does, for whom, why people should buy from you, what kind of place it will be to work in. The more the company has a real character, the more people will be prepared to subsume personal interests to company ones. In the old days troops were led into battle, and possible death, under a standard, an emblem that was laden with history, value and meaning. Fortunately your people won't be under quite as much pressure – but have a standard for them anyway.

Have a culture of success. Visualise success, and make sure your team does the same. Celebrate success whenever it happens.

Professional sports people do this, visualising success via videos of their own greatest moments, and celebrating outrageously whenever they succeed again – hence all the hugging and kissing after every Premiership goal. Can you create a similar feel in the office? Much of British culture relies on the subtle put-down, meant as much in friendship as in enmity – we're encouraged to be modest about success. Try and create a different feel in your start-up. When the first big order comes in, go crazy!

Celebrate success whenever it happens.

Your Dream Teamers are 'doers', remember, so encourage this. Have a can-do culture, where people get praised for having a go at something. If the start-up is busy, there will be more jobs to be done than people to do them, so let people have a go if they think they are 'up for it'. Clearly this has to be within limits, but you're sensible enough to know these.

Of course, if you do this, it's only a matter of time before somebody makes a mistake. The single best way to demotivate Dream Team players is to make them feel small and stupid because of this (especially if the humiliation is public). If you feel angry and tempted to do this, resist the temptation. Count to ten; get working on damage limitation; tell the culprit not to worry. Later on, talk privately to the individual. If they don't know already, point out what they did wrong. Ask them how they think they could have handled it better. If they don't have good answers, provide them yourself. End the interview on a positive note. We all make mistakes; there's lots more stuff to do and get right. Don't create victims.

If someone regularly goofs, then they may need more watching. You must have taken them on because you thought they had qualities. Were you wrong? They may have to move back into a more structured environment. Make sure they don't leave feeling bitter, otherwise you've got an enemy out there.

Two virtues not given enough coverage in the leadership books are *politeness* and *clarity*. Business mythology is full of successful 'bastard bosses'. We have no idea how true these myths are – though our perception is that these characters are particularly effective at generating short-term profits in growing markets. But even if there are some great bosses who are bullies, don't use that model in the start-up. It's too small a place.

Clarity is a much undervalued management virtue. Tell people what they are supposed to be doing and why. This sounds obvious, but surveys often reveal managers to be mired in uncertainty about what the hell their actual job is. Their superiors' excessive use of management-ese adds mightily to this confusion.

Most important of all, you must *lead by example*. The stuff above won't really work if you are seen to be moody, aggressive, cynical, capricious or devious. Look in the mirror every working morning and remind yourself that you are going to be leading people today. They will be following your example.

Leadership on a beermat

★ Select wisely

★ Set clear rules

★ Have a vision (and communicate it)

★ Have a culture of success

★ Be clear and polite

★ Lead by example

Beermat.biz

How do you want them to be? Be that way yourself. It's amazing how the thought of this responsibility can curb the worst side of your character and – here's the real prize – bring out the best.

If you want to know how *not* to do it, get some videos of the TV series *The Office*.

Here are some other observations about the nature of start-ups...

Perhaps the single most obvious trait of the start-up is its *DIY mentality*. In an established corporation, there is a set way of doing almost everything. In the start-up, there are no set ways of doing anything. Just get them done!

Music is a useful metaphor here. The corporation is a symphony, with parts neatly written out for each instrument and a conductor to keep them together. The start-up is a small, improvisatory jazz band: the intrapreneur has scribbled a few chords on the back of envelopes and handed them round. He or she counts everyone in, and after that everyone is relying on their skill, imagination, attention to the other players and the sudden demands of the musical situation, moment by moment.

Start-ups are under *perpetual cash pressure*. This is often made worse by some entrepreneurs' passion for spending money on showy irrelevancies that 'make important statements about the brand'. We advise all start-ups 'out there' to get a finance cornerstone on board as early as possible, and the same should be true for the start-up intraprise.

Entrepreneur David Hall says that entrepreneurial teams have to 'beg, borrow and befriend' when they start. Can you get something for free? Can you barter for something you'd otherwise have to pay cash for? Can you borrow an asset, even for a weekend, to get a particular job done?

This may be new to corporate people, who even in these cost-conscious days expect a certain level of support and quality around them. But it must be accepted. For most successful start-ups, those early, cash-strapped days become treasured parts of the mythology. Enjoy the adventure!

Note that, while this may sound cheapskate and vaguely embarrassing to people used to corporate ways, it should be good news to at least one person in the corporation – the CFO. Start-ups have acquired a reputation for being expensive: one of the key purposes of this book is to disprove this. Endless technical tinkering and excessively abstract market research can make start-ups expensive, but it doesn't have to be that way.

The one cost of intraprise that you cannot get round is the opportunity cost of having able people working on the projects – but this is essentially an HR (and, ultimately, a strategic) issue, not a finance one. We believe the payback in terms of motivation and development well outweighs this cost.

And note that team members are only expected to work *part-time* on an intraprise, until it gathers real commercial momentum. Start-ups 'out there' usually begin like this, with a team of part-timers (or maybe one full-timer plus part-time cornerstones). Arguably they all should: people with too much time on their hands can waste it fiddling around with non-essentials.

It is vital that the team be given some company time to work on the new project. 3M famously allow intrapreneurs to spend 15 per cent of their time on pet ideas. At the other end of the scale, we have been saddened to be on excellent innovation sessions, where teams have come up with brilliant ideas and an innovation manager has allocated small but sensible budgets to them – whereupon the winners are told that their line managers insist on having them back, doing their old jobs exactly as before. This effectively kills intraprise for anyone with a family or who wants a life outside the workplace.

Start-ups are also under *time pressure*, and this is also healthy. Good start-ups get the product in front of the market as quickly as possible. We say 'in front of', because this isn't about rushing products out. It *is* about talking to the market as soon as possible. In *The Beermat Entrepreneur* the future sales cornerstone was on the phone to some favourite customers the morning after the first pub brainstorming session, not to sell anything but to chat, and in the process, to gauge interest. The new company kept a low formal profile till the first order came in.

Good **start-ups** get **the product** in **front** of the **market** as **quickly** as possible.

If you are entering new markets, start in a similar, informal manner. Is there someone in the corporation who knows the market you are looking at? Someone who has joined recently from that sector, perhaps… If not, which bit of the corporation comes closest to that market, either as a customer or as a supplier? Someone there will have useful knowledge, and hopefully even contacts they will share with you once they trust you. They may have market-research material that covers the area you are interested in (they bought it for another section of the material). And, of course, keep talking to your sponsor to see if he or she has contacts there.

Once you have a few 'beachhead' contacts in that market, go and talk to them about the product. Find out if it really does solve 'pain' for them, or how it could be amended to solve that pain, or who else really does have that pain, in spades (it's amazing what people will tell you if they have nothing to lose by doing so and if they like you).

That's how successful start-ups do valuable market research, at no financial cost.

All sounds great, doesn't it? In the next chapter we shall look at some of the pitfalls intrapreneurs have to negotiate and the special skills they need in order to do this.

Life in the start-up

★ Powerful, tribal culture

★ Hard work

★ Fun!

★ 'DIY' mindset

★ Relentless cash pressure

★ Part-time to start with

★ Must get to the market as quickly as possible

Beermat.biz

Chapter Five: Here Be Dragons

Some people think that being an intrapreneur is 'like being an entrepreneur, only easier'. We hope we've already sketched out ways in which there is truth to this statement, but there are also a number of ways in which the intrapreneur's life is harder.

There's a bestselling book on negotiating called *Getting to Yes*. The intrapreneur dreams of having a chance to get *near* yes: much of their time is spent 'getting past no'. Often they have to sneak past no, and only ask the question when the 'yes' is a *fait accompli*. This is not easy.

The main problem is the nature of most corporate (and public-sector) cultures. The old adage that 'nobody ever got fired for buying IBM' still reigns in big organisations: rewards come for not making mistakes, rather than for taking risks that work out.

Entrepreneurs, on the other hand, live in a world dominated by risk. The intrapreneur has to straddle these two worlds, or rather create an alternative world half-inside, half-outside the organisation, and weave in and out of these two worlds. Hence the desperate need for high-level sponsorship in the risk-averse corporate world.

Some corporate readers may object that they are no longer as risk-averse as they were ten years ago. This may be true, but there is still a long way to go. The dot-com madness did not help here – it has provided stacks of 'told you so' material for risk-averse senior managers. It is the main purpose of this book to provide a logical, structured way of dealing with risk, and thus a counter-argument to the 'told you so' brigade. We quite agree: the dot-com era was a farce. Here's how to do intraprise properly.

Also, within even the most go-ahead organisations, there will be individual pockets of resistance to intrapreneurship. Here is a list of the kinds of dragons you may need to slay, or at least sneak past, on your way to intrapreneurial success.

Clever nay-sayers. A cult of 'clever negativity' can develop in big companies. People want to appear intelligent (or are intelligent, and want everyone else to see that). One way of doing that is by coming up with clever arguments *against* things. Usually the arguments *are* clever – plain stupid arguments won't cut it – but they actually miss the point.

Our culture values and fosters critical thought, which is on balance a good thing. But it can become a burden if misapplied. In the entrepreneurs' environment of high uncertainty, faith and determination are of more use than rigorous critical thought. A culture that values cleverness above all else might sound like the ideal breeding ground for new technologies and businesses, but can lead to 'paralysis by analysis'. A healthy dose of irrational gung-ho is essential.

On the other hand, it can be necessary to point out potential hazards to overenthusiastic intrapreneurs! This should be done by asking questions – 'how are you going to get round the X problem?' – rather than via brilliant put-downs that help nobody except the ego of the speaker.

The way to deal with clever nay-sayers is to stall them. Take note of any objections they make. Don't leap in with a reply;

just say it's a good point and you'll come back later. Go away and think about it. Talk to your sponsor. Come up with the right answer. You may end up thanking them for pointing out a problem, against which you are now forearmed.

Some clever nay-sayers like playing psychological games, getting less brilliant people annoyed, then criticising them for having a bad temper. Don't fall for this. Stay cool. If you are pressed for a reaction at once, insist on having some time. If you are cornered by such a person in a meeting, do the same: the other people in the meeting will understand.

Get back to your own people, and reconnect with their enthusiasm. Remind yourself that it's not clever words that create great businesses, but imagination, belief, personal skills and hard work.

Get **back** to your **own people,** and **reconnect** with their **enthusiasm**.

Green-eyed monsters. Jealousy can be a major force within large organisations. It will begin the moment the intrapreneur is given any time off to pursue their idea (and they must be given this time). Sensible fellow employees will say: 'Good old Fred, at last he's been given the chance to try one of those ideas he's always on about'; or 'Brilliant, at least someone around here is making waves. Let's hope it makes us all rich'; or, best of all, 'Hey, I'd like to get involved in that project too. How can I help?'

Actual reactions will vary across a rather wider spectrum, from the sunny ones above, through unconcern, to downright antipathy. This antipathy may well come from people more senior than the intrapreneur – a particularly dangerous occurrence. And if it is the intrapreneur's line manager, there can be a real problem.

Jealousy can make people surprisingly devious, so it is usually hard to spot them. Othello didn't have much luck rumbling 'honest Iago'. Use your intuition – a much underrated business tool.

Confronting jealous individuals directly is never fruitful. They'll just deny it or, worse, get into a 'mind-game' by accusing you of making false accusations against them.

In all cases, if you come to the conclusion someone is sabotaging your efforts out of jealousy, the first person you should talk to is your sponsor. They may be able to get the person in question off your back. If the saboteur is your line manager, then you should be out of that department anyway – they're not going to work with you, develop you, give you room to grow. At least you now know that. You may have to shelve the intraprise for the moment until you can find yourself a proper 'springboard'.

Former nay-sayers. Another source of antipathy to a new idea is people who have already rejected it. Apparently people who join those cults that predict the end of the world on a given date are often even more convinced of the cult's message once that date has passed and everyone is still happily going about their business. It's a psychological defence against looking stupid. 'The Master just got the date a bit wrong,' they say, fixing you with a crazy stare. 'Just you wait till *next* Friday 13th'.

As we've said, marketing departments are often the culprits here. They don't usually have the crazy stare, but their research showed that there was no market for this product, and they're the experts!

Luckily these people are easier to deal with than the jealous. For a start, you probably know who they are, while the jealous ones lurk under cover of niceness. And secondly, their emotion is less strong than jealousy, and thus more open to rational conversion.

Nevertheless, you might as well steer clear of them if possible. If you must deal with them, go and talk to them direct. Ask for a few minutes of their time. Before you speak to them, take a moment to clear any resentment from your own mind. Think open, honest, forward-looking, positive. Is there any way in which you have put their past negative input to positive use? If so, start by thanking them for it, and explain how you have acted on it. Are there any other changes you have made since they were so scathing about your project? Play up the changes. In the worst possible case, you just have to rely on a simple request: 'I know you were against this idea, but we're giving it a try, and we need your help.'

Know precisely the deliverables you want from them, and ask for these. Most important of all, resist any and every temptation to score points off them, even if they try and set you up to do this.

Resist any and **every temptation** to score points off them,

Carthorses. Large organisations are full of people we call 'carthorses'. They have been with the company since joining as indentured child labour back in the mid-19th century, and now have a small fiefdom, which they run adequately well. They probably have only a handful of years till retirement, which they intend to serve out in their fiefdom. The last thing they want is some smartarse barging in and doing stuff like changing things or borrowing their people for a 'wild' new project.

There's not much you can do with these people. Appeals to their adventurous spirit will fail, since this, sadly, died in them decades ago. Open conversations with them will probably end with: 'I'm not letting you bugger things up round here, and that's final. Now, if you don't mind, I've got work to do...'

Your sponsor may not be able to help, either. The carthorse may actually have done a good job over the years, and will certainly have allies throughout the business, who could make even the sponsor's life a lot more difficult.

As with the green-eyed monsters, you must find a way round carthorses. If you go into a head-to-head with one, you will at best expend huge amounts of energy, and at worse set a whole network of powerful people against you. The key here is not to let your pride get involved. Admit it: this old bruiser could beat you if it came to a straight fight. So don't get into one.

Much better to bypass the carthorse. They're pretty static, so it shouldn't be that difficult. Your sponsor may well know other people who have come up against X and found a way past them.

Once you do get past them, don't be triumphalist – however tempting it may feel. As for entrepreneurs forced out of their companies, the best revenge is to have a happy life, or in your case a successful intraprise.

New CEOs reading this might be tempted to set up some slightly cocky intrapreneurs to flush out all the really backward-looking carthorses in their organisation. Of course, we'd never suggest such a devious course of action…

Short-termists. According to the school of thought led by Will Hutton (*The State We're In*), short-termism is the curse of British business. They point to Japanese companies that draw up 50-year plans, or to Zhou Enlai's famous comment about the French Revolution (when asked what he thought its consequences had been, he replied, 'It's a bit early to tell').

The City certainly takes too short a view of things, with trustees breathing down the backs of fund managers every quarter. We're not so sure about business as a whole. You know your company – does it really think long-term?

If the answer is yes, then it is a fertile ground for intraprise. If the answer is a loud no, then you have a problem. Your task is going to be harder. But don't despair. The chances are that someone, somewhere near the top of the organisation, has made critical comments about this. Find out who, and arrange to meet them. Will they act as your sponsor? It could be extra-fun, a bit like plotting a revolution. Yes, it'll be more risky – plotters sometimes end up getting executed – but if you're an intrapreneur, risk isn't something that puts you off, anyway.

Often short-termism results from an excessive influence of a certain type of CFO. It's worth talking to this person, pointing out that if you follow the methods recommended in this book, intraprises do not consume vast amounts of cash. He or she may still be equating intraprise with dot-com extravagance. Do them a favour and update them.

Rescuers. A more subtle destructive force can be unleashed on the new venture by individuals purporting to be its friends.

They have meetings with you, discuss stuff, but nothing ever seems to materialise; always, of course, for perfectly good reasons way beyond the rescuers' control. At best the meetings just waste time, but at worst these people can be very draining of energy. Their mating call is 'I'm only trying to help' (accompanied by a rather hurt expression) – a sign to thank them politely for their input and look elsewhere for assistance.

According to Transactional Analysis (yes, we know it was a fad a few years back, but actually it has a lot to say), some people spend a great deal of time playing out the roles of Rescuer, Persecutor or Victim. They tend to move round the 'drama triangle' created by these three, by suddenly switching from one role to the other, usually via some 'scene'. The spurned Rescuer who goes off in a huff has switched to Persecutor; the Rescuer who leaves you feeling guilty at your lack of gratitude for his or her help is now probably being a Victim.

If you think this is a bit 'pop-psychological', look at the popular press, which makes hard cash (and lots of it) out of the drama triangle, setting people up as rescuing heroes one day, and persecuting them as villains the next.

The brand police. Unlike the fire-breathers listed above, we have sympathy with these dragons. There is a real issue here, which many intrapreneurs blithely argue away – totally incorrectly. Big companies don't only own great brands, they *are* such brands themselves, and they must protect the value of them.

One can get very metaphysical about brands, but we prefer to stick with the basics: they are indicators of trust. And trust is incredibly valuable. This is why huge sums are spent 'building brands' via various media, when actually all this does is get the product on the starting line to become a brand. (Ten years later, once millions of people have bought the product, loved it, found it reliable and consistent, and now trust it implicitly to work – well done, you really have got a brand.)

Sadly, brands can be damaged a lot more quickly than they are built up. Instances of great brands going 'downmarket' abound, and always end in tears. So the one thing a big and highly respected corporation does not want is gimcrack products appearing with their name on it. Enthusiastic intrapreneurs often talk about 'leveraging the brand', but should you do that with an untried, untested product? Answer, of course, is no.

There will in every business be individuals who see it as their duty to prevent the corporate brand 'going downhill'. How does the intrapreneur deal with them?

Firstly, they must be respected. They are right to worry. They must be convinced that the intraprise is not going to adulterate the brand.

The way *not* to do this is to rave about the new product and how wonderful it's going to be. You don't know it's going to be wonderful; you just believe it will be. The brand cops probably reckon the opposite. They may be right.

What you must do is convince them that you are a responsible guardian of the corporate brand. Here are two pitches to a customer:

One: 'Megacorp Advanced Solutions. New ideas, with all you expect from Megacorp.'

Two: 'We're from Megacorp Advanced Solutions. We've got this great idea for a grommet, which we think will solve your grommet problems for good – once we get it working, which we hope you will help us do. This is not a standard corporate offer, so doesn't come with the level of perfection you've come to expect from Megacorp. It's an experiment. Of course, we're all Megacorp people, so we have the same standards of integrity: you know we're not wasting your time…'

One may sound snappier, but it's just this kind of thing that the brand police are terrified of – and rightly so, in our view. Convince them that you will be using the second approach.

You must mean this, too, and not lapse back into overusing the brand once you have persuaded the cops to let you have a go. Your sales cornerstone may well start nagging you to do this – think of all those leads! – but you have to resist.

If the answer from the brand police remains 'no', despite your clear and genuine commitment to uphold the brand, then you may have to try a more radical approach. If the parent company is excessively brand-conscious, the start-up will have to be independent as soon as possible. No mention of the parent should be made. Behind the façade of independence, you should still use company assets wherever possible, but to the outside world you are not part of the brand.

Overeager suits. This is more of a problem for later-stage intraprises. You're up and running – doing rather well actually. The doubters have long been silenced. You also know that there will come a time (we talk about this later) when you have to hand over the business to more conventional corporate managers. But that's still a long way away. Right now, there are only eight of you… You're summoned to the CEO's office; you assume for another pat on the back, like last time. And you're told, 'Well done. You've done a great job. It's time for you to hand over to a more experienced management team.'

This is a disaster. It is not time to hand over. It's far too early. But a decision has been made.

The experienced managers move in. They quieten the place down a bit – set more rigorous financial targets and get rid of those jeans, those erratic hours and that rather wild salesperson, whom the customers liked, but who tore up the rule book.

Shortly afterwards, sales begin to dip. More resources are thrown at the product, with some proper market research and product development. The research still doesn't demonstrate a big enough market and, while the development irons out a few problems (which, actually, no customers had complained about), the improved product doesn't really fit into the firm's existing distribution system, so it still doesn't sell. Losses start to mount: finally the decision is taken to close the new business. More than one person mutters that they told the CEO so…

Conspiracy theorists spot evil forces at work here – or at least empire-building. But this can happen with the best possible motives. The shoestring enterprise was doing well, the argument ran; time to reward it with some proper resources.

But it was not time, any more than a start-up 'out there' of that size should fire its cornerstones or suddenly look for huge tranches of venture capital. The time for that is much later (more on this in Chapter Eight). Sending in 'big management' too early destroys the culture, flexibility, spark and sheer bloody irrationality that are essential to developing great new businesses.

There is also an information transfer issue. The new suits rarely pick up the right information when they arrive. The team have learned a great deal about the new business in the time they've been running it. The new arrivals rarely have the humility or the time to sit down and really learn this stuff and, even if they did, they might not get told it, partially out of irritation, partially because much learning is subconscious: the departing people wouldn't know what knowledge to pass on.

If you are the unfortunate intrapreneur in the above story, talk to your sponsor at once. Try and get a stay of execution, and marshal your arguments – feel free to quote from this book, and from the section on 'Handoff' in Gifford Pinchot's classic *Intrapreneuring* text. Get your most corporate-minded, rational team member to present these arguments. It's worth the fight.

Dragons

★ Clever nay-sayers

★ Green-eyed monsters

★ Former nay-sayers

★ Carthorses

★ Short-termists

★ Rescuers

★ The brand police

★ Overeager suits

⊚Beermat.biz

Sponsors and pro-intrapreneurship CEOs have to face dragons, too. Here are some arguments used against an intrapreneurial culture.

Management have other things to do than to listen to crackpot ideas from people who should be concentrating on their job.

This is particularly used against initiatives such as the Beermat Intrapreneurship Workshop (see pages 114–116) and other effective listening schemes. But good listening schemes all have inbuilt 'anti-crackpot' controls. (In our model there are two: the fact that teams – not individuals – come up with ideas, and the fact that people then have to present them live to their peers – the sight of a team that has decided to take the mickey out of the process marching confidently onto the stage, then dissolving into blushes and apologies, is always rewarding.)

What is true is that some ideas that emerge from these processes are a bit small-scale. However, almost all have a logic to them, and they are all important to the person suggesting them. Even the person who suggests watering the tobacco plant in reception more often has at least gone through a process of thinking about the business, and will now feel better for having been listened to. And may even save the plant (it has been looking a bit yellow at the edges…).

One must also question the suitability of a manager who makes this kind of comment – why do they have such a low opinion of the 'crackpots' who work for them? Because their people are genuinely stupid? Or because they are stupidly managed?

OK, this stuff may be good for motivation, but we all know that most 'good ideas' turn out not to work.

Exactly. That is why the intrapreneurial process in a company has to be done in the right way. The purpose of the methodology we propose is to test new ideas *quickly, cheaply and quietly*. 'Take risks, make mistakes quickly, fix them fast', to quote management guru Gary Hamel. You don't need huge committees poring over business plans. You do need a quick decision – from the only judge that really matters, the marketplace. And don't forget: some ideas *do* work. Here are some famous quotes, gathered from various sources.

'The wireless music box has no imaginable commercial value. Who would pay for a message sent to nobody in particular?'

Bosses of David Sarnoff, 'the father of broadcasting', while he was a junior at Marconi

'I think there is a world market for maybe five computers.'

Thomas Watson, chairman of IBM, 1943

'There is no reason anyone would want a computer in their home.'

Ken Olson, president, chairman and founder of Digital Equipment Corp., 1977

'This "telephone" has too many shortcomings to be seriously considered as a means of communication. The device is inherently of no value to us.'

Western Union internal memo, 1876

'The days of groups with guitars are over.'

A and R man at Decca Records in 1962, turning down a tape from a new pop act called The Beatles

'It is difficult to identify particular applications for which this is unusually well suited... so cannot recommend pursuing it.'

Major consulting firm asked to evaluate the new copying technique of xerography in 1959

▶▶

'Aeroplanes are interesting toys but of no military value.'

Marshal Ferdinand Foch, Professor of Strategy, École Supérieure de Guerre

'Everything that can be invented has been invented.'

Charles H. Duell, Commissioner, US Office of Patents, 1899

Beermat.biz

Oh, and here's one of our own. *Beermat* was top of the entrepreneurship bestseller charts for more than a year and is still selling well. We sent the manuscript to a range of publishers, two of whom came up with the same one-word description: 'Unpublishable'.

Feeling better?

Back to our objections…

We're too big. A start-up won't deliver the growth we need.

If you set up a new business and it's so successful that after two years it's turning over £20 million – that's amazing. Except in a £5 billion corporation, where that £20 million is a drop in the ocean. If the corporation wants 10% growth where's the other £480 million coming from?

The scale argument is initially powerful, but not fatal to intraprise.

If you get the new business really right, it can turn into a major profit centre on its own. The Sony PlayStation was an intrapreneurial project: by 1999 it had bought in $6.5 billion in revenue, at margins three times higher than Sony's core electronics business. OK, not every intraprise is going to turn out that way – but don't forget Goldman's Law. You just don't know! Even if, after five years, the new unit is earning £100 million, that is hardly insignificant. And once you have several smaller but real successes, their effect is cumulative.

There are also a host of 'knock-on' advantages from intrapreneuring, which we shall discuss fully in Chapter Seven.

But aren't entrepreneurs a pain in the neck?

That's a polite way of putting it. The answer is often 'yes'.

*Intra*preneurs are more likely to have had a few of their jagged edges knocked off by corporate or shop-floor life, but they are still likely to be the mavericks around the place. But the point about these people is that their strengths hugely outweigh their weaknesses – as long as these strengths are managed properly.

Isn't this just another fad?

We believe not. Remember that almost all great businesses begin life as enterprises. Dust down your corporate mythology.

In the end, there will always be a few unbelievers. As long as they don't sabotage innovation, and do what they do well, then they can be lived with.

Chapter Six:

Intrapreneur Skills and Advantages

Hopefully the last chapter will have scotched the myth that intrapreneurship is easy. It isn't. In this chapter we'll look at some of the specific skills you need in order to slay dragons and build great intraprises. To lighten the load, at the end we'll also list some of the advantages that intrapreneurs hold over entrepreneurs out there 'in the wild', and show how to leverage these as effectively as possible.

Beginning with the skills... What do you need, over and above the 'standard' entrepreneurs' toolbox?

In a sentence, intrapreneurs need to manage their superiors, ally with their equals, inspire their subordinates, and network with everybody.

Manage your superiors – political skill. This is a requirement from which the 'wild' entrepreneur is mercifully free. You are not so lucky. Your first, and most important, political task is finding the right sponsor. Your next is continuing to work well with your sponsor. The more dealings with senior people that you can channel through your sponsor, the better.

However, there may be times when you have to handle objections or ask for favours from senior people, and your sponsor is not around. In these situations, honesty is the best policy. Have a clear idea of what you want from someone, and ask for it openly, backing up your request with rational, not emotional, arguments. If the person is obstructive, stay calm, end the meeting politely and go off to plan a new strategy for getting what you need.

You should be building an 'institutional map'. Quietly gather all the information you can about the company, its structure and people. Make sure you know if there are any implacable opponents of the intraprise, and plan routes round them if possible. Find out who might be potential allies. Journalists are masters at this kind of map-making: emulate them.

Always be polite to PAs, assistants and other links between you and people at the top, whether their boss is a potential ally or not. Yes, this 'skill' is standard good manners, but people often ignore it, nevertheless.

Intrapreneurs need to manage their superiors, ally with their equals, inspire their subordinates, and network with everybody.

Ally with your equals – social skills. Useful as allies 'up there' can be, it is very often people at your own level who are your best helpers. This is because much intrapreneurial work is done in 'stealth mode'. If you can simply get the use of a machine for an evening by asking the works manager rather than by going via the Chief Operating Officer, then it's both simpler and more fun. The latter point is actually important. If people are told to cooperate with you, they probably will. If people think that cooperating with you is a bit of an adventure, they will not only cooperate but get involved. Especially at the early stage of the venture you must be on the lookout for allies – people who have the right technical skills, and who also have a touch of buccaneering spirit about them. They may even be potential cornerstones.

Inspire subordinates – motivational skills. We've already discussed this in the section on culture (see page 69–73).

Supposing you really don't feel you are leader material? Arguably you shouldn't be running a start-up, but if you do find yourself in that situation, lead as well as you can. The most important things are to keep the vision alive – keep reminding yourself and your colleagues of the purpose you are working towards – and be polite and clear in your dealings with everybody. This will get you a long way.

Network with everybody!

Networking is an essential skill for the intrapreneur – as it is for the entrepreneur. Get to know as many people as possible, in as many parts of the company as possible. Keep business cards, and make notes on the back about the person. Take the time to send a 'nice to meet you the other day' email – assuming it was nice. You must be sincere. If you really didn't like the person, but think they 'might be useful', that's a recipe for being let down at a crucial moment.

Don't restrict your networking to the company. Attend industry conferences, get to know counterparts in other businesses. Technical people are often particularly good at this –

many a friendship has sprung up over a pint of two of real ale, discussing the merits of new technology and the demerits of current and past employers.

Networking
is an **essential skill**
for the intrapreneur

And don't stop there. Innovative ideas often come from 'recombining' problems, technologies, business models or skills from different areas. The wise intrapreneur should have the curiosity of a toddler, and should keep an eye perpetually open for what people in other industries are up to.

At the same time as you network in person, consider online networking tools (see page 111). People tend either to love or hate these – find out which category you fall into.

As you build a team, ensure they network too. They do not have to do so as widely as you – if their network remains in their field, that's fine. But make openness and communication part of the culture.

The intrapreneurial advantage

Here are some of the advantages the intrapreneur faces, when compared to his or her counterpart trying to set up a business out 'in the wild'.

A range of mentors. In the first edition of *Beermat*, we argued that you should only have one mentor, otherwise wires would get crossed. On reflection, this is not the case: you'll probably have one special mentor to discuss the most important and personal matters with, but 'specialist' mentors for particular topic areas. Why not?

A customer mentor is particularly valuable. If you are attacking Quadrant 3 (yes, this is getting to sound like *Star Wars*), the people who know best what other 'pains' you could be solving are the people with that pain, your customers. So go and talk to them. If you have a good relationship with a range of customers, the chances are that one or two will be personal friends, or at least people you like. If you are a sales cornerstone, who do you really look forward to visiting?

Buy this person lunch, and talk the new ideas through. Be honest: say you are looking for advice from them. If you have chosen well you can get hugely valuable information.

What motivates the customer mentor (apart from the free lunch)? As with your sponsor, it begins with the fact that you like one another. If the customer is in a structured middle-management position, there may be the additional excitement of being at least tangentially involved in a start-up. And if the product turns out to work as well as you hope, he or she will gain kudos within the company for bringing it in before rivals got hold of it. As usual, always be thinking 'win-win'.

Supposing you are planning a direct sell to the consumer? This is a much harder kind of sell, in our view, but if this is your choice, your external mentor could be an *intermediary mentor*, someone in, say, retailing who really understands market trends. This kind of mentor is particularly helpful for Quadrant 4 start-ups (see page 35).

A customer mentor is particularly valuable.

You are still at an advantage over an entrepreneur in finding such a mentor: someone else in the company may recommend you, or at least you can use your company name to get you past the front door.

Customers within the organisation. You might find a customer mentor elsewhere in the organisation. You may find actual customers here, too. Why not? This isn't a 'cheat' – they will only buy if you save them money, time or effort: this way the company benefits twice over.

The corporate network provides other benefits, too. We have mentioned the 'Rembrandts in the attic' phenomenon. Are there any other pieces of *Intellectual Property* you could turn into businesses, or use to make your business more efficient?

A key question you need to ask as you network is, 'Where's the slack?'

Where is there a machine lying idle, an empty office, a bored IT person with time on his or her hands? Or, best of all, a budget underspent and needing to hit a target by (fast-approaching) year-end? Of course, none of these things would exist in the perfect company. In every real company staffed by human beings, not robots, they abound. Intrapreneurs become very good at sniffing them out.

'Where's the slack?'

One of the biggest problems faced by 'wild' entrepreneurs is access to *prototyping facilities.* They design something on paper; they may run up a model in their potting shed; but the materials aren't right and it doesn't begin to do the idea justice. The idea dies, mouldering in the corner of the shed till the inventor's partner throws it away or it gets cannibalised for the next brilliant idea. The intrapreneur should never have this problem. Companies switched on to intraprise should provide prototyping facilities. Dinosaur companies won't provide this – but the savvy intrapreneur will get networking, talk to a few technical people, and get the job done somehow.

Premises are another nightmare for entrepreneurs. For the intrapreneur – no problem. You should have a workplace already. If you are an office worker, there's a phone, probably an internet connection, copying facilities… Every day you can stroll into your office, pause by the water cooler for a nice long drink, say a little prayer of thanks and think of all those aspiring entrepreneurs in damp basements or sitting at home while their teenage son practises Jimi Hendrix's louder solos.

Later on we argue that the intraprise should find its own premises as soon as possible. The team needs to be 'colocated' (a wonderful piece of management-ese we spent ages pondering, till we realised it simply meant that they work in the same place). But that still takes us back to the question 'Where's the slack?' The company will have something somewhere.

Entrepreneurs seeking to 'colocate' the team have to go through the hell of dealing with commercial estate agents. Once again, be thankful.

As well as premises, there are many other support functions that you come to take for granted in a big company, but whose absence hits you like an Arctic gale the moment you step outside the corporate environment. Legal support, for example. The well-networked intrapreneur need only pick up a phone (or at least get his or her sponsor to sort something).

As always, the secret is to network, network, network, so that you have a web of allies in various parts of the firm – and outside, in its customer base – all of whom like you and think the new idea sounds fun. Then use them wisely. Never call in too many favours: these are busy people, remember, and your attraction is that you make a bit of a change from the routine. As Tolstoy said, 'Influence is a capital; once squandered, it cannot be regained.'

On that classy note we'll end this chapter. In the next chapter we want to look at things from the CEO's perspective. We hope we made the point right at the start of this book that it is hugely in the big corporation's interest to foster intraprise — as long as it manages it in the right way. In Chapter Seven we look in more detail at how this pays off, examine what 'Innovation Incorporated' might look like, and make some comments about motivating intrapreneurs. We shall also look at some alternative methods of creating new businesses from within the corporation.

Chapter Seven: The Boardroom Entrepreneur:

Leading Innovation from the Top

What would 'Innovation Incorporated' be like? Not a free-for-all, with everyone chasing the latest crazy idea. Our model intrapreneurial corporation is still busy in its traditional core markets, improving existing products and services and keeping an eagle eye on changes in those markets.

Around the time of the dot-com boom, management gurus started quoting Che Guevara or Mao Zedong ('Bomb the headquarters!'), in the belief that the internet had propelled business into a totally new era, when all the old rules would be ripped up. Even Jack Welch got a bit net-heady, setting up an initiative called 'destroyyourbusiness.com', which assumed there were internet entrepreneurs a mouse-click away from blowing all GE businesses out of the water. The company soon concluded that this was an illusion: the net was more about helping existing businesses do what they do better. The initiative was renamed a gentler 'growyourbusiness.com'. Needless to say, the first initiative got a lot more media coverage than the second.

Nevertheless, there is an element of revolution in what we are proposing – a quiet, slow-burning revolution, more like the Industrial Revolution than anything courtesy of Lenin or Mao. Its patron saint is more Joseph Schumpeter than Karl Marx.

The Boardroom Entrepreneur begins with a shift of priorities. *Intrapreneurs* are now important people. The company must help them, empower them – not so that they can waste resources on zany ideas, but so that they can build ideas using a rigorous, tested methodology. The company will sit in judgement on the ideas as little as possible, leaving this to a better judge: the marketplace.

But this isn't just about intrapreneurs, or even intrapreneurs and their teams. *Everybody else in the business* should feel more involved, more 'listened to', more a part of an adventure. (Everybody? Of course, some people will opt out, as they do from any big change…)

The key to this general involvement is to create a system of seeking and implementing suggestions that actually works. We know that the track record of suggestion systems is historically dreadful, but believe strongly that this has been because they have not been of the right kind, or taken seriously enough. It is imperative to get these systems right, for three reasons:

★ they yield invaluable information

★ they are hugely motivational

★ they involve everyone in innovation, and thus defuse potential envy of successful intrapreneuring teams.

More on this topic below.

How should the company look, function and feel?

Organisationally, a glance will reveal little change. The existing divisions are getting on with what they usually do, though a look at their accounts reveals a new, but still small, venture budget. This budget is minute compared to the hundreds of millions thrown at 'venturing' by some companies. Are there swathes of new job titles? No, only for a handful of people.

Yet beneath that, there has been a big shake-up.

This **budget** is minute compared to the **hundreds** of millions thrown at '**venturing**' by some **companies**.

Venture Units. Many companies have set up special units that manage the venturing activity of the whole business. These often have substantial budgets, and are looked on as potential saviours of mature companies. While this is probably better than taking the ostrich approach to the changing marketplace, they do not have a great track record.

By their very existence, special Venture Units bracket venturing off as a special activity that some people do and others don't. This can easily create envy, a 'them and us' feeling that is fundamentally contradictory to the true spirit of the company, whereby (almost) everyone is a participant in change.

This is particularly true if:

★ lots of money is thrown at this unit…

★ …while everyone else has to soldier on under tight financial controls

★ the unit operates with a high level of secrecy

★ the unit produces reports in management-ese

★ the unit gains a reputation for scoring 'clever' points off people who present ideas to them.

If change becomes something you have to have an Armani suit and an MBA to do, then the spirit of innovation is under threat.

If the Venture Unit becomes another hoop through which intrapreneurs have to jump – life presents enough of these, anyway – then it is failing its fundamental role, which is to evangelise innovation.

We've heard it said that 'The prime job of Venture Units is to filter (and kill off) bad ideas'. No, no, no. That is the 'job' of the marketplace.

It is the job of the Venture Unit to help intrapreneurs and their teams win that battle. It should be trying to make it as easy as possible for intrapreneurs, so that they can save their energy for the real war, in the marketplace.

It is the **job** of the **Venture Unit** to help **intrapreneurs** and their teams **win**

There is also a considerable danger to the 'filter' model, namely that the 'experts' in the Unit will get it wrong. Remember Goldman's Law – and reread pages 90–91 if you need further inspiration.

We propose an alternative, 'enabling' model.

Mimicking the marketplace

Supporters of the 'Venture Unit as idea filter' model argue that 'in the wild' entrepreneurs have to jump through hoops, in the form of capital providers, so intrapreneurs should have to do that within the company. Yes, but...

Firstly, we argued in *The Beermat Entrepreneur* that entrepreneurs should avoid reliance on capital providers and, where humanly possible, *fund from revenue*. Those three magic words should also be the mantra of all intraprises. (Of course, it's not always possible, but it's amazing how 'possible' that becomes once the determination to do so is strong.) More on this in the next chapter.

Secondly, 'out there' there is a *competitive marketplace* in capital provision. If one lot turns you down, you can try somewhere else. So a monolithic Venture Unit that has life-or-death powers is not a mirror of the world 'out there', but a mirror of just one part of that world, an individual capital provider. ▶▶

Supporters of the 'filter' model will argue in return that the corporation will almost at once be overrun with ideas, most of them crazy. We have more faith in intrapreneurs. There is, anyway, a natural filtering system, just as there is for entrepreneurs. In *Beermat* we talked about 12 'hurdles' that a new entrepreneurial idea has to cross in order to turn into a great business. Intraprises face hurdles, too. Initial ones are all to do with people. If the intrapreneur cannot attract a sponsor or cornerstones, the idea will wither away. If their sales cornerstone talks informally to their favourite customers (for a Quadrant 3 idea) or some new customers (for a Quadrant 4 attack) and they all express disinterest, the venture is – not dead, but definitely 'back to the drawing board'. If the prototype keeps falling apart, the idea is on hold till either the innovation or delivery cornerstone solves the problem.

Rather than a specialist, centralised venturing budget, there should be competing pots of money, earmarked for venturing. These should be spread around the company as widely as possible, to mimic the 'natural' environment faced by entrepreneurs. Each department should have a small venture budget, as should 'fellows' (see page 120).

Beermat.biz

What should the Enabling Venture Unit be doing? The answer is 'whatever intrapreneurs need'. Some obvious ones…

★ *Prototyping*. Savvy intrapreneurs often get prototypes made on the quiet, either by themselves or by a colleague. Nonetheless, if some form of 'Intraprise Workshop' were available, where someone was on tap to help intrapreneurs create prototypes, this would be hugely useful.

★ *Information*. It would be useful to have someone who knew who in the corporation was working on what, as they might be able to suggest areas where people could work together. This function would not extend to ordering intraprises to ally, or, if there were duplication, telling one intrapreneur to stop: nothing wrong with a bit of internal competition! But it is useful to know if there is someone else in the San Francisco plant working on the same stuff, so that you can choose whether to compete or ally.

This function should extend to knowledge management – marshalling and disseminating all the learning produced by intraprises. The many intrapreneurial forays into various markets will all yield information. Who is talking regularly to intrapreneurs and cornerstones, collating this information and making it available to other people in the company? As with many Venture Unit functions, this would operate in parallel with more informal processes and networks.

★ *Idea circulation*. R and D often come up with 'interesting things they don't really know what to do with'. Often these just end up in cupboards. Then there are all those inventors in the company, hard at work in their potting sheds. All these ideas would be gathered in – the inventors possibly via competitions – and circulated round the company, for intrapreneurs to consider. It's a formal way of doing what evangelists (see page 32) do.

A classic example of this is the Post-it Note. We tell the story in greater detail in Appendix A, but right now the salient fact is that when Spencer Silver invented the semi-sticky glue that makes the note work, 3M circulated the idea round the company. Art Fry, an intrapreneur, latched onto it.

★ *A marriage bureau*. The Venture Unit should have lists of intrapreneurs and potential cornerstones, and ensure that they all meet regularly to discuss ideas, projects, and so on. They can also be more pro-active, suggesting that particular intrapreneurs and cornerstones meet.

★ *Services*. The best intrapreneurs 'beg, befriend or borrow' to get the resources they need. Being the people they are, they will no doubt carry on doing this. At the same time, certain services could be provided centrally. Legal ones, for example. Company lawyers working on big corporate stuff may not be so familiar with the issues facing start-ups: the Unit could have access to a specialist. For premises, a list of currently vacant properties could be kept. Yes, the best intrapreneurs will sniff out much of this stuff anyway, but why not have back-up?

★ *Cultural events*. Enterprise culture, that is. The Unit comprises the right people to liaise with in-house Enterprise Clubs (see page 112) and organise workshops or speaker evenings, where successful entrepreneurs, intrapreneurs, cornerstones, business angels, enterprise gurus (etc.) pass on knowledge, tips or simple enthusiasm. Why not start a business book group for top intrapreneurs?

★ *Exchanges*. Proven intrapreneurs could be sent on exchanges with other companies in different business sectors, to get fresh perspectives.

★ *Monitoring the transition*. This is the one piece of formal management that the Unit does – and even here, it should only do so in close cooperation with the individual sponsors and funders of each intraprise. There comes a time in the life of the most successful intraprises – between their having 20 people and their having 40 in the business – when they go through a massive culture change, from a tribal start-up to a more solid business. All enterprises have problems negotiating this stage: the Unit can help here.

The issues at this time centre on the intrapreneur and cornerstones: are they adapting to the new environment? There's no formal way to test this, but colleagues and the sponsor are likely to know. The Unit should be talking to all intrapreneurs and cornerstones, and watching for '20 to 40 transition issues'. If these issues do arise, they must be dealt with – tactfully. The Enabling Venture Unit is not allowed to turn into a macho, heavy-handed filter over this one issue. More on this transition in Chapter Eight.

The kind of cultural, supportive work the Enabling Venture Unit does might not appeal to a certain type of graduate who thinks that business is about strategy creation, drawing diagrams, sounding clever at meetings, and so on. Such individuals have a lot to learn, and an Enabling Venture Unit would be a damned good place for them to start doing so. Really intelligent graduates will get the point, enjoy the work and get involved in lots of great new business ideas. It could be a route to the top.

Encouraging sponsorship. Alongside the essential work of the Venture Unit, a second strand of intrapreneur assistance should be available via a means totally invisible on the org chart: sponsorship. We've already talked about how this works (see Chapter Three), so won't go into it again. What matters here is that the company actively encourages sponsorship.

There's an interesting debate as to whether this should be via financial rewards or not. We're tempted to say not (another way in which the intraprise revolution is invisible). The best sponsors do so because they love it, not for money. Monetising the reward might attract the wrong sort of people. There are many other ways in which a Boardroom Entrepreneur CEO can boost sponsorship…

★ Job specs should allow 'natural' sponsors time to do this important work.

★ The most successful sponsors should be there in the Hall of Fame, alongside the successful intrapreneurs.

★ A simple 'Well done' to someone who's put time into an intraprise can be embarrassingly important.

Hall of Fame? Yes, we know it sounds very American, but we Brits should be ruthless in copying all good ideas from across the pond. Rolls-Royce have a fine museum telling the story of the company – its two entrepreneurial founders; its greatest technological leaps; the best pieces of corporate mythology, such as the night a motley crew of RR employees worked all night to get a seaplane ready to compete in (and win) the Schneider trophy.

What **matters** here is **that the company** actively **encourages sponsorship**.

The worst Halls of Fame feature endless portraits of chairmen or managing directors. They tell no story; they feature no designers, sales people or (Heaven forbid!) shop-floor people. They are about as interesting as watching already dry paint remain dry.

Our Hall will tell the company story, featuring heroes and heroines from all levels of the hierarchy. Leaders, of course, but also engineers, marketing people, the man who set up the grommets division in 1963, the cleaner who revived a visiting Japanese businessman who had suffered a heart attack (and so on...). Everyone featured will be there on merit – they did something special for the company. At the end there will be empty spaces, ready to be filled. And maybe a list of current intrapreneurial projects, their teams and status.

If in doubt, think theme park rather than museum. It's about getting everyone to understand the adventure the business has been, and to share in the even greater adventure that is to be its future.

Communication. The Hall of Fame is one aspect of a key priority: communication. This has become a bit of a cliché – it's hard to find any organisation that will stand up and say, 'We're rubbish at communication, and we don't care.' But in practice it is still done better by some businesses than others. You need to do it brilliantly.

Some ideas...

★ *A live intranet*. 'Out there' entrepreneurs are networking on the net, via portals like Ecademy (check it out on www.ecademy.com). These portals have become very sophisticated (and, as they do so, easier to use – following the Advantage Timeline and moving beyond those nerdy early adopters to a larger, early majority user base). They aren't just message boards, but have clubs you can join, levels of membership and correspondence-tracking features. The fundamental philosophy of these portals is to enable people to talk to one another, not to direct conversation. Ecademy clubs, for example, are founded and run by members, not by any of the site staff. It is low-cost, because the participants do much of the work – and have fun doing so.

A common fear expressed is that all kinds of bad stuff will go on through these clubs. This is a piece of silly old prejudice about the net. OK, so a 'we hate the company' club starts up. Get in there and see what people are complaining about. Are they right? When you reply, don't use a piece of corporate PR; get someone to enter into a dialogue with the complainants.

There may be the odd spat about 'netiquette' being breached, so there will need to be someone in overall charge to moderate proceedings. Ideally someone selected by the participants, not by you. But essentially these things self-police. Anyone who's being a complete wanker will be told so by the other users.

★ *Networking meetings*. Online networking only goes so far, however. Beyond that, people must meet and talk. This may be one-to-one; or it may be in club meetings. The firm should have a two-pronged strategy here: clubs that spring up naturally should be given encouragement; at the same time, why not set up specific clubs – technology, inventors, intrapreneurs, a business discussion forum – and see what happens? Clubs shouldn't be seen as the monopoly of people who network via computer: company-founded clubs break this monopoly. Note that the clubs formed via the intranet needn't be business-related. Who knows, from your beekeepers' club a revolutionary new lightweight construction technique might emerge, which will sweep the world market…

★ *A decent company newsletter.* This is another hoary old favourite in need of revitalisation, not binning. The fundamental problem with company newsletters is that they communicate one-way, whereas people are now used to internet-style communication, which is interactive. Communication is more about listening than talking – remember those rather smug comms lecturers telling you that you had 'two ears and one mouth' (just in case you'd suddenly forgotten and started trying to shovel food up your nose…). As a result, the more the newsletter spouts the company line, the more cynical readers will be about it and the less they will bother to read it.

Clearly you don't want to foment Trotskyism or tell everyone that the opposition's products are better, but why not run debates about company policy or give the union rep a column? And, of course, have a page for intrapreneurs. Your company is a dynamic place, full of bright, decent people: reflect that. Get everyone to share in the adventure.

The same goes for other kinds of traditional internal communication. There's something to be said for an annual pageant oozing confidence – but the rest of the time err on the side of treating people as equals.

The most important aspect of communication, however, is a suggestion scheme that really works. A method for running such a scheme is presented in the box overleaf.

Note that only a subset of ideas generated will be fully intrapreneurial. Most will be to do with incremental improvement to current processes. These can be hugely valuable – after all, the people making these suggestions do this stuff every day. Even if the ideas prove unworkable, as long as the suggesting team is told why they can't be implemented, there will still be motivational benefits.

The Beermat Intrapreneurship Workshop

Get groups of your staff into a room – 50 or so at a time is ideal. Then give them a talk about how entrepreneurs find and develop ideas. The materials we use are the 'Magic Question' and the 'Original Beermat' (see Chapter Eight), which requires them to come up with an elevator pitch, a sponsor for the idea and a first customer. Then split them into about eight teams, and send them away to imagine they are groups of entrepreneurs/cornerstones in pubs, asking first, 'Where's the pain?', then brainstorming ways of solving it. We find it is best to keep the scope open – anything is fair game, from the minutiae of internal process to the wildest leap into Ansoff Quadrant 4.

Each team has to draw up a shortlist of 'pains' and solutions. These solutions must be given the 'Beermat' treatment – elevator pitch, sponsor, first customer. For the moment, the sponsor can be anyone they think would take on the job: to suggest the CEO is fine, though most people tend to look closer to their own boss's level. The first customer must be a real customer for an imagined product or, for an internal process idea, a section of the business where it can be trialled.

Once everyone has come up with these, get them to gather again, and ask each group to present their three favourite ideas to everybody else.

The group nature of the proceedings is very important. Because people have formed into groups and discussed the ideas, those ideas become property of that group, thus spreading ownership of the best thought. The group nature of the process also weeds out the worst ideas.

Management must be on hand, to provide immediate feedback. Three types of reply are needed:

★ Gold is an *immediate 'Yes,* we'll do that!' As simple as that.

★ Silver is a *qualified yes.* The idea sounds good in principle, but there are other people who need to be spoken to.

★ Bronze is a *'No, because…'* A reason must always be given for deciding not to action an idea.

There is sometimes a 'wooden spoon', too, where people are larking about and come up with an idea they know to be ridiculous. This does no harm at all, as long as it is a one-off – have a laugh about it, then get on with the more serious business.

A public record must be kept of all ideas and of the management response. If the idea is Gold or Silver, ▶▶

a follow-up chart must be kept. For Gold ideas, this need only say when the idea was formally actioned; for Silvers, the chart must show what has happened – either action or rejection. In the latter case, an explanation needs to be available to the idea generators.

This saying 'why' is hugely important. In so many suggestion schemes people are not told this. The idea just fades away. This leaves employees deprived of key information that might help them go away and reformulate the idea more successfully, as well as giving them a vague feeling that they have stepped out of line by coming up with this stuff in the first place – and could they now shut up and get on with what they are paid to do. Not exactly motivational!

Every session should be followed up three and maybe six months later, with a management report on how the idea is working. The team can discuss further 'tweaks' to the change if necessary. Clearly, if the ideas prove not to work, this is the time for them to be demoted to Bronze – and, as above, for the generating team to be told why.

Suggestion schemes are far too important to ditch. They are an essential mechanism for communicating with the workforce, for motivating them and for giving you valuable information about your business. But they must be done properly, in company time, with management behind them.

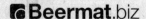

Resource allocation

It is here that commitment to intrapreneurship will be most tested.

Intrapreneurs need access to all kinds of resources over time, but the two crucial ones that they must be given formally are time and money.

Time. We place this first because this is the most important.

We've already mentioned the tragedy of the intrapreneurs with the great idea, who get a pat on the back from someone very senior in the company and a small budget to go and develop the idea – then return to a dragon line manager who says, 'No, you can't take any time off my work to do this other stuff.'

One definition of leadership is 'setting priorities', and it's clear that in the above example the wrong priorities have been set: 'Be intrapreneurial, as long as it doesn't upset the status quo.' It's no use having intraprise as a kind of fun optional extra, on a par with the works bowling team. It must matter, and be seen to matter.

On the other hand, everyone in the company has jobs to do, and must do them. People can't sit around 'being revolutionary' all day: this is a 21st-century corporation, not the Sorbonne in 1968 or a dot-com in 1999.

Initially, it's a good discipline for intrapreneurs to have to do most of their early work in their own time. Ideally, their line manager will 'cut them a little slack', on the agreement that if the intraprise begins to take off, he or she will get credit for having done so. Why not have bonuses for managers from whose departments come the largest number of successful intraprises?

In addition, why not have a yearly allocation of paid 'intraprise hours' that everyone can spend on projects? 3M expect staff to spend 15 per cent of their time on their own projects. We're not sure you have to be that generous, but you must allow a reasonable amount of time.

Beyond a certain stage, intrapreneurs and their teams need to be able to go and negotiate with their divisional heads an allocation of time to spend on specific projects. The role of the Venture Unit would be to help them present their case, not to judge them – though, of course, if the Unit people consider the idea poor, they will end up saying so. This is legitimate, as it is not the same as having the power to kill the idea. Plenty of 'informed' people tell 'wild' entrepreneurs that their ideas are crazy. Wise entrepreneurs listen to the reasons why – then either decide to make changes to get round the problem, or jump back into their Panzer and charge on anyway.

You must allow a reasonable amount of time.

Over time, decisions as to how much time to give intrapreneurs will become easier – as intrapreneurs build up a track record. 'It's another of Jim's ideas. His last two worked brilliantly. Give him extra time.'

As well as this, there must always be room for new people with new ideas.

The Beermat model of entre- and intrapreneurial development provides an objective yardstick, not of 'how good an idea is' (only the marketplace will tell you that), but of how far an idea has moved down the line from 'lightbulb going on in intrapreneur's head' to world domination. This is a useful tool for assessing how worthy an idea is of company time.

There must **always** be room for **new** people with **new** ideas.

Money. Money is the less important of the two key resources. You can build a great business without inputs of capital, by *funding from revenue*. You cannot build any business if you don't have the time.

Sometimes it is impossible to fund totally from revenue, in which case measured amounts of capital are required. The job of allocating it within the corporation should be easier than the task faced by capital providers 'out there'.

Sadly, the level of trust and communication between entrepreneurs 'out there' and their capital providers is generally appalling. There's often an unbridgeable temperamental and cultural gulf between passionate, impatient entrepreneurs and process-minded bankers or Venture Capitalists.

In the *intra*preneurial context, this gulf should not exist. On the intrapreneur side, he or she is less likely to be quite as wild as the entrepreneur. The intrapreneur will have some idea of how resource allocation in the company works, and may even know the individuals making the decision. On the other side, the internal capital provider may know the intrapreneur or, if not, can talk to the sponsor. Bankers and VCs may have niggling worries about the trustworthiness of their clients; this should not be the case within the company. And, of course, the whole operation is less risky anyway: money is not being transferred from one institution to another – essentially this is an internal debate about budgets.

Yet it is still important to get away from the 'Venture Unit as filter' model. Funding is perhaps the main area where Venture Units can build themselves up into becoming major venture-stifling bottlenecks, and this must not be allowed to happen.

We have already alluded to how to prevent this – mimic the world out there and have competing sources of finance within the company. The savvy intrapreneur will probably have played a bit of this game anyway, finding a small training budget they could use for a test run of the project. But the company needs to make this arrangement formal.

One way of doing this is to give each major business unit an intraprise budget. This must be to hand out to intrapreneurs, not for division heads to fund pet projects.

Another idea is to have 'bursaries' available. These should be available to anyone who can assemble a team of at least:

★ intrapreneur

★ one technical cornerstone

★ sales cornerstone

★ sponsor.

The bursary should be small – to encourage frugality, but also to ensure that plenty are given out. And their distribution should be in the hands of as many people as possible, to ensure as wide a spread of attacks on markets. Gifford Pinchot argues that companies should appoint 'enterprise fellows' to do this – ideally people with a good track record as sponsors, but possibly also successful intrapreneurs, or (when the project is starting) anyone the CEO thinks is interested in fomenting entrepreneurial culture.

Pinchot also calls for building up 'intracapital'. Once new ventures have begun to create returns, a proportion of this should be retained to fund more enterprise. More radically, successful intrapreneurs should keep a portion of these funds, not as personal wealth, but as budgets for new projects.

We'd like to conclude this section with a reminder that innovation does not have to cost a fortune.

Given the uncertain nature of entrepreneurial markets, the overriding need is to have as many forays into them as possible. These do not have to be expensive: the Beermat methodology is all about quick,*cheap* and quiet tests of ideas. Remember also that many entrepreneurs 'out there' build up companies almost totally funded from revenue – and not just service companies, either: biotech companies can fund drug development by having a services arm. (We met an excellent pharma company in Scotland doing exactly this; Millennium have done something similar in America.) The key to successful intraprise is reminding yourself of these facts, and being acutely suspicious of 'Corporate Venturing Plans' that insist on huge capital outlays before anyone really knows if any of the products have got what it takes.

innovation does **not** have to **cost** a fortune.

Any other comments about the 'feel' of the kind of corporation we envisage? Clearly, such a business is not plagued by short-termism. This may be easier said than done, if the City is breathing down your neck – but you will have to stand up to these people, so start now. Make it plain that you have a clear strategy of innovation in place, which you are going to stick to. Investors hate uncertainty, so they will at least respect your clarity on this. Don't make unrealistic promises to them. This may sound obvious – but not long ago a UK utility company 'promised' the City 15 per cent annual growth for five years. We wish them well with this, and hope they are empowering their intrapreneurs to the max. The City is notoriously unforgiving of people who promise and fail to deliver.

This company is not dogged with a 'blame culture', which has been the curse of many British institutions. Americans seem to understand much better that hardly anyone gets everything right, and that failures are actually steps to success – except for people who refuse to learn. The opposite of the blame culture is not somewhere you can make any balls-up you feel like making, but a 'Learning Organisation' where mistakes are examined and learned from, and the learning is then disseminated throughout the business for everyone's benefit.

Finally, a reminder that IP needs to be at the heart of strategy. Those dusty Rembrandts are valuable! The Chief Patent Officer should be a senior person, and it should be one of their key duties to help intrapreneurs select projects.

This **company** is **not** dogged with a '**blame culture**',

Other approaches

We think that you can't beat empowered internal entrepreneurs building businesses from within the company.

But there are other initiatives that can create value – as well as ones that, in our view, destroy it.

Bringing in entrepreneurs. Entrepreneurs from outside can come and work with the company on projects. This may either come about if an entrepreneur approaches the company directly, suggesting a strategic alliance, or if you go out and recruit people. Either way can work.

Some businesses are excessively weighted in one direction, usually technical. There may not be any intrapreneurs around – only inventors. If this is true, attempts at intraprise end up with groups of inventors arguing about features. These people need an entrepreneur to turn their ideas into businesses. If there are no such people within the company, as with any shortage, buy some in.

However, entrepreneurs are unlikely simply to want to stay on the company payroll — their feet are too itchy for that. They may also want a bigger upside than the corporation can provide. So set up a joint venture.

In *Beermat* we recommended that entrepreneurs form strategic alliances with big companies, if at all possible. For them it provides (or should provide) many 'intrapreneur' benefits, such as access to customers and to potential cornerstones, an office and a measure of corporate back-up. For the corporation the main benefit comes if the entrepreneur has a really good idea and business model to go with it. Other benefits are inspirational – potential intrapreneurs get to meet and work with a real live entrepreneur – or PR (big firm seen to be working with small business rather than screwing them, which is, sadly, often the public perception).

The brand police may well express concern that the entrepreneur will abuse the brand to promote themselves – as with many business issues, this is about judgement. Only form alliances with entrepreneurs whom you like and trust.

Corporate Venture Capital. There was a craze for this around the dot-com boom, when real live VCs appeared to be making shedloads of money. Now realism has returned to the market, and VCs are sitting on portfolios of dud investments – as are their corporate counterparts.

Venture Capital funding is best left to experts. Oddly enough, this is particularly true if you are trying to create an intraprise culture in your business. VCs' approach to enterprise is too sceptical. Many years ago classic VCs such as Arthur Rock were like business angels, taking equity in return for money and support. Now it's all about money. You do not want to be like this.

Supposing you are approached by a company wanting a VC-style investment from you?

If they are in an area that your business understands, then consider a joint venture, where you are effectively acting like a business angel, proving capital *and* support.

If they are in an area that your business knows nothing about, it is hardly responsible to throw shareholders' money at it.

There are always exceptions to this advice – GE Capital has been a huge success. But note that it has remained resolutely unglamorous, sticking to pure or relatively pure financial plays like insurance or leasing, not throwing money at sexy-sounding but untested technology.

Proponents of 'CVC' argue that it can be used to seed markets, to create a 'buying infrastructure' for a company's products. Microsoft and Lucent have both invested on this principle. Will this pay in the long run? Our feeling is that if you can't run these businesses as joint ventures, then you are too far from them and it's not a wise use of shareholders' capital. The billions that these companies have spent on 'strategic CVC activity' could empower a lot of intrapreneurs.

Winning through intraprise

When talking to the City, nothing will convince it better than your own conviction that this strategy is right. Here are some reasons why you will emerge a winner.

Strategy. All strategy is about gaining long-term advantage over rivals. Can there be a better way of doing this than by having a range of subsidiaries that grow into leaders in their markets? Especially in new, dynamic markets… All competitive advantage erodes over time: by creating great companies in new markets, where competitive advantages are easier to secure, you maximise your chances of remaining a 'growth company'.

To the strategist's question 'Which market shall we attack next?', you answer, 'As many as we can.' Initial attacks are with guerrilla forces; beachheads are established easily, cheaply and quickly (or, if not, lessons will be learned about the hidden difficulties of these markets).

Critics say this might produce a rag-bag of companies, but our guess is that intrapreneurs, who are experts on your company and its products, will naturally start looking at adjacent markets and technologies. If these are already being covered, intrapreneurs will look a bit further afield, but they still won't stick pins into a map of the economy at random.

The image is of rhododendrons colonising a patch of ground. Most clumps simply grow bigger and take up more space. Some roots disappear underground and shoot up in new areas. Later on, as both this new shoot and the parent expand, the gap between them shrinks, till finally they are united. Other roots go a long way underground, then surface to become patches of colour that never merge with the parent above ground but still flourish. A fourth kind of shoot, of course, fails to take because the ground it enters is unsatisfactory. Often that ground remains barren – if this busy, colonising plant can't conquer it, nothing can.

As well as covering a lot of ground, the plant changes the entire ecosystem of the area. You do this, too. Huge synergies can spring up between intraprise (or between intraprises and the parent company). You will also acquire totally new customers or suppliers, who will hopefully realise what a good company you are to do business with. As you enter new markets, your people will expand their network, thus presenting more opportunities.

Knowledge. The gain in the company knowledge base is of enormous value. Indeed, some people argue that this is the most important benefit of intraprise. Who was it who said that 'The only sustainable source of competitive advantage is a company's ability to learn'? Intraprise creates fantastic learning opportunities.

Interesting as abstract market research is, it is no substitute for actual people trying to sell products or services. Perhaps the guerrilla metaphor should be changed to an espionage one: your intrapreneurs in Quadrants 2 and 4 are your eyes and ears in a whole range of new markets. You will also have access to

Intraprise creates fantastic learning opportunities.

much subtler, better-tested knowledge about your existing markets, from all those intrapreneurs who chose to attack Quadrant 3.

Clearly this knowledge needs to be managed. This, as we've said, is a key task of the Venture Unit. Knowledge management is still developing, but there can be fewer more interesting challenges for a knowledge manager than the one of regularly debriefing intrapreneurs and their teams about their markets.

The company's technology and skills base will be broadened, too. The imagination of innovation cornerstones (or intrapreneurs, who often fulfil this role) will be set free to tackle new problems. Delivery cornerstones will develop new processes and practices to meet the newly discovered needs of customers (or the needs of new customers).

There are great stories about intrapreneurs dragging huge companies kicking and screaming into a new technology: two examples (read the stories in Gary Hamel's *Leading the Revolution*) are the team who switched IBM onto the internet, and Ken Kutaragi, who led Sony from analogue to digital technology via his intrapreneurial PlayStation. Two rather fortunate moves, we reckon.

Here is another area where IP strategy and intrapreneurialism go hand-in-hand. Intrapreneurs won't just be rummaging through the attic looking for Rembrandts; they will be creating new works of art to join them (hopefully not too many dead sheep or beds littered with condoms…). The cost of patenting means that maybe not every patent can be filed, but it is wise to invest here, and have a policy of 'If in doubt, patent'. Inventor intrapreneurs are notorious for inventing something, finding it doesn't quite suit the current purpose, forgetting about it, then a couple of years later suddenly realising that it's exactly what they need for a totally new challenge.

Motivation. Another huge win from a correctly applied strategy of intrapreneurism is improved motivation. Obviously intrapreneurs, cornerstones, intraprise Dream Teams and sponsors will be given a huge boost. But the Beermat Intrapreneurship Workshops will be taking the message to everyone in the company that the management respect their point of view, are genuinely listening and want them to be involved in the adventure as much as possible. Added to this, there should be a buzz around the company, with its many new directions and ventures. Certainly, with small companies, you need only walk into the office to sense how things are going. The winners hum with energy. Be like that, too.

One major problem facing big companies is the retention of bright people. You spend a fortune recruiting them, another fortune training them – then they leave, apparently dissatisfied with the 'level of challenge' in their work. A spell as an intrapreneur or in an Enabling Venture Unit could be exactly what they need. The challenges are never the same from one day to the next (one intrapreneur described the experience as 'an MBA every day').

An intrapreneurial company is also more likely to attract bright people in the first place, both from among graduates and, more useful still, from among experienced people in rival companies, who look across at what you are doing and decide that the grass is definitely several shades greener.

One **intrapreneur** described the **experience** as '**an MBA every day**'.

Leadership. Spotting and developing the future leaders of your business is one of a Boardroom Entrepreneur CEO's most important tasks, if not *the* most important one. Intraprises are great places to do this. People who create and build intraprises are natural leaders: they have vision, charisma, motivational skills. They also *develop* leadership skills in the process. The intrapreneur has to look at his or her business as a whole, to coordinate the efforts of a team of specialists in the business, to think strategically. A spell at the helm of an intraprise is an important part of the training of your business's next generation of leaders.

Note that some intrapreneurs do not wish to become corporate leaders – see the material on motivating intrapreneurs on page 136. These people should not be forced into the boardroom against their will.

Efficiency. An intrapreneurial company is an efficient company. Firstly, those Beermat Intrapreneurship Workshops will come up with many ways to cut waste – from the people who see the waste every day. The brightest suggestions may even come up with ways of turning that waste into a product!

An **intrapreneurial company** is an **efficient company**.

Starting in 'stealth mode'

Intrapreneurs dreaming of an enterprise revolution sometimes believe that if only the CEO wanted change sufficiently, he or she would order it, and all the dragons would damn well have to obey. The reality, of course, is harder. Divisional heads dislike diktats from head office, especially if they involve extra cost (they resent head office costs enough as it is…). And intrapreneurship does have a cost, initially mainly that of time.

As a CEO committed to a quiet revolution, how do you bring it about? Quietly, of course. Intraprises themselves start best in 'stealth mode', and the quiet revolution should do the same. So don't announce a company-wide programme. Yet. Our guess is that at least one divisional boss gets the point of intrapreneurship. Talk with him or her, and set up an informal project there.

Aim for a 'quick win'. The best route to this is to add service. If it must be new technology, is it something you could license out early rather than develop all the way to market (especially in Quadrant 4, where the markets are unfamiliar)?

Once one of the new ventures is bringing in some cash, then you have a story to tell everybody else and can set about a company-wide launch. Sceptical divisional heads will be more likely to accept it when you say those magic words, 'This is an investment, not a cost', and have a story to tell that proves it.

We reckon you have three years from the announcement of an initiative to the point where a critical mass of opposition destroys it. So delay the formal announcement, and make sure there are potential quick wins in the portfolio.

Should you lie to people in the pre-announcement period? Being fans of ethical business, we prefer not – but must leave that one to you in the end. Machiavelli would have lied, for the greater good of the corporation. Gandhi would not. You know your style of leadership.

Beermat.biz

Secondly, intrapreneurs are always on the lookout for slack. An idle machine, an empty building – savvy intrapreneurs will nose these out and put them to use. In firms used to big, 'lumpy' projects there can be a great deal of slack: this is an ideal way of putting these assets to use.

The structure of the intraprise

What is the best format for intraprises? We believe that the answer is to make them as like 'wild' start-ups as possible.

Give them their own *premises* as soon as possible. Just as entrepreneurs have to start off by blagging office space, so the intraprise can begin in an empty office somewhere. As soon as possible the team should be working from their own location.

They should have their own profit and loss account as soon as possible, too. For a while this will be distorted in their favour, as they 'beg or borrow' assets from the parent company. But, just as you try and set adult standards for a semi-dependent teenager, so the start-up needs its own measures of financial performance from day one.

At the same time, the start-up should not be given the tight financial *targets* that the rest of the company has to live with. It just can't meet these in the same way that existing divisions can (or should), and to expect them to is destructive. Instead, the intraprise should be seen as having milestones – hurdles to leap over (or fall at), just as enterprises do.

In *Beermat*, we listed 12 hurdles between having the idea and 'world domination'. The 12 on the next page are similar, but slightly tweaked to fit the challenges facing the intrapreneur, who has to overcome more inertia and do a lot more politics.

Note that serious, formal Business Planning does not occur until late in the process. This may horrify some readers, but don't forget Goldman's Law (see page 16). With an entre- or intrapreneurial venture, there is no point in going into complex and time-consuming planning exercises until a real feel for the market has been acquired – which can only be done by actually selling things to people and finding out what benefits they are prepared to pay for. As we've already said, the market is very unlikely to respond as you expect it to.

Another contentious area is *recruitment* – when should the intraprise be allowed to recruit externally? If there is an IP issue, then the answer may be 'not for a while', but otherwise the answer is 'as soon as they like'. We've already talked about

12 hurdles for the intrapreneur

1. The intrapreneur has the idea.

2. The intrapreneur 'falls in love with the idea'.

3. Sales and finance people agree to join the team.

4. Approached informally, customers express interest.

5. A senior person in the company agrees to become the sponsor.

6. The Founding Team is complete.

7. A 'customer mentor' buys a prototype/trial run.

8. The customer is happy – a White Paper is prepared.

9. Ten more paying customers are found.

10. These customers are happy.

11. A 'Real Business Plan' is drawn up.

12. Sales targets on that plan are met (and expenditure kept 'reasonably under control').

Beermat.biz

selective recruitment of 'wild' entrepreneurs to turn groups of technicians into business teams. If the intrapreneur is attacking a new market and knows a salesperson who is expert in that area, then why not have this person as sales cornerstone? Note that we say 'knows' rather than 'knows of': recruiting cornerstones must be done on a personal basis.

When it comes to the Dream Team, recruitment should still be by personal recommendation. This will tend to mean attracting people from within the company, but does not necessarily mean so. Of course, an outsider will have to be paid a salary from day one, whereas a company person can be seconded for a while before taking up a permanent post, so internal remains best. And it is in the company's interest to second bright young people to intraprises, as they will learn a lot there. Ideally there would be no external recruitment to a Dream Team, but in practice a measure of it will cause no problem. It's probably best to keep 'insiders' in the majority, though.

Once the business gets beyond 20 to 40 people, it will be taking on 'employees' and must be free to source these from wherever it decides is best.

To whom should the intraprise *report*? A really radical answer is 'nobody'. More practically, the answer varies during the life of the intraprise.

At the very start, of course, the answer is genuinely 'nobody'. The intrapreneur is still working on the idea, floating it past friends, maybe designing a prototype or chatting, totally informally, to a few customers. If things don't work here, the project will probably get shelved anyway. If anyone is 'responsible' at this stage, it will be the intrapreneur's line manager, who may have been asked for a little time off to work on the idea. He or she should check, informally, with the intrapreneur how things are going.

If the idea does appear to have 'legs' – some customer interest, a prototype that looks feasible – the next individual to be reported to should be the sponsor. 'Reporting' will still mean informal chats rather than anything structured.

Responsibility broadens if there is an appeal for money. Innovation Incorporated will have decentralised 'fundholders': departmental enterprise budgets, a range of 'enterprise fellows' offering bursaries. Clearly once the intrapreneur and the team secure funding from one of these sources, they are under a more formal duty to report progress to them. Note that at the same time they must keep the informal communication going with their line manager and their sponsor.

The next crucial phase comes when the intrapreneur and some of their team need to be working full-time on the project. Here, for the first time, a senior management decision may be required. There should be 'intraprise sabbaticals' available, but these have to be decided formally and from on high. The ideal person to be in overall charge of this process is the CEO, though in practice they will need a 'Venture VP', whose job it is to keep him or her up to speed with all the major (and as many of the minor as possible) intrapreneurial initiatives currently under way. But the person with the power must be the boss.

In practice, the Venture VP will wield quite a lot of power, as their recommendation will influence a busy CEO. But the more attention the CEO can pay to intraprises, the better.

Lovers of corporate organisation may consider the above model messy. Yes, it is messy, because the real world of enterprise is messy, and our model says that the corporation should follow the pattern of real-world enterprise as closely as is sensibly possible. We do not see there is danger in this. The intrapreneur's sponsor and department head will be keeping an eye on things, and later on a fund-giver, the Venture VP and the CEO. There are plenty of checks and balances.

It really boils down to a philosophical question: what is management anyway? Is it rigidly steering a business down a narrow, clearly defined channel, or is it a light hand on the tiller, watching out for 'drifts into error' and correcting them gently and calmly before they become endemic and serious?

Structure. What form should the intraprise take – spin-off, subsidiary, joint venture?

The answer is, as always, 'It depends', but the default position should be a simple business unit, wholly owned by the parent company. An alternative idea, of having an 'almost wholly owned' subsidiary with a small chunk belonging to the founding team sounds attractive, but can lead to accounting difficulties. It is probably best to reward successful intrapreneurs and their team with bonuses (related to the performance of their start-up) and stock options in the parent company.

Later on it may be decided to 'spin out' the business, either via a Management Buy-Out or a trade sale. In the former case, the managers suddenly become potential owners. We say 'potential' as MBOs are usually organised by Venture Capitalists, who are noted for tying managers up in contracts that make their prospective ultimate wealth appear larger than it ends up being. If things go even slightly off plan, the whole outfit can end up belonging to the VC.

In some cases the new unit will be a joint venture, either with another company or with an entrepreneur, in which case ownership will be a matter of debate between participants.

Motivating the intrapreneur

Remember that intrapreneurs are entrepreneurs who choose to stay in large companies. The dream outcome for them is being given opportunities to create new businesses – with your assistance – while retaining the financial safety and the 'belongingness' that comes with membership of a large organisation.

Opportunity. This is probably the greatest single motivation for the intrapreneur. If they come up with a great business idea, you're going to give them time, space and support to turn that into a reality. The intrapreneur will flourish under these conditions.

Challenge. Given the opportunity, intrapreneurs will enjoy the process of capitalising on it.

Freedom. Too much control will switch off their natural flow of energy, commitment and enthusiasm. That is why a loose, informal, advisory kind of reporting is best. How much freedom should they be given? The answer is, of course, more and more as they prove themselves. This 'more and more' can be reflected in the amount of budget they can requisition without examination, and the extent to which they can leapfrog the power structure and talk, if not to the CEO, at least to their Venture VP.

Respect. Entrepreneurs seek respect, and so do intrapreneurs. Remember their initial motive is to change the world, or at least a corner of it. By giving them opportunity, challenge and freedom, you set up this most important motive. Once the change is in motion, they want to be recognised for what they are doing. Hence the Hall of Fame, with its emphasis (but not total concentration) on successful intrapreneurs.

These are the main drivers. But what about those two corporate favourites: career and money?

Intrapreneurs are not immune to the charms of these, but the benefits above greatly outweigh them.

Career. The intrapreneur may have an eye on the top job. In which case they will have to re-enter the standard career path. But for many intrapreneurs, a career means more, better opportunities to start businesses. Other, more 'corporate' lures might include an enterprise fellowship, with bursaries to hand out (and a major mentoring role with it), or the chance to go on an exchange with a totally different business to learn how it works ('thinking inside a new box'). Or, of course, the leadership of the Venture Unit, a post probably best handled by an experienced intrapreneur (though it would also be brilliant training for a bright high-flyer…).

But the true intrapreneur is probably happiest building businesses, so should be left to get on with it, getting more and more scope and more and more respect each time they clock up a win.

Money. Naturally entrepreneurs want to make money, but changing things, and being recognised as having changed things, are more important still. The same is true for the intrapreneur. So he or she should receive a healthy bonus for getting a successful intraprise off the ground – as should their team. This can take the form of cash, parent-company options or, ideally, both. In the dot-com era, people asked for stakes in the new company, but there are catches to this. There is no reason to suppose that the start-up will ever be sold, so what is their stake worth? In those heady days, successful spin-offs were rushed to public market, but this rarely happens nowadays. A verbal promise of a stake if the company ever does go public is perhaps a good 'sweetener', but that's all it is.

So the reward for the intrapreneur boils down to giving them the opportunity to start businesses, freedom to build businesses and respect when the businesses succeed. Plus a bonus and/or parent-company stock. For some intrapreneurs there is an added incentive that the board is noting their successes and is thinking of reintegrating them into the 'ladder' at a new, higher level.

Arguably, intrapreneurs reward themselves anyway, by doing work they love. Maybe all you're really doing is enabling them to do this – the most important thing an inspirational leader can do.

Dramatis personae

A reminder of the key players:

★ The Boardroom Entrepreneur: the CEO, driving the whole process

★ Divisional head who 'gets the point' and will run the pilot

★ Venture VP

★ Sponsors

★ Venture Unit – enabling, not filtering

★ Other divisional heads, allocating divisional enterprise budgets direct to intrapreneurial teams

★ 'Enterprise fellows', controlling enterprise bursaries

★ Intrapreneurs

★ Intrapreneur foils

★ Intraprise cornerstones

★ Intraprise 'Dream Teams'

★ External entrepreneurs, working on joint ventures with company teams

★ Intrapreneurs from other companies on exchange with your intrapreneurs

★ Everybody else, on the lookout for ways of doing things better, and knowing that if they formulate and present suggestions based on these in a clear manner, they will be listened to.

Beermat.biz

The HR perspective

Alert HR professionals will have been reading this chapter and commenting that much of what is contained there is *their* business, on a day-to-day basis, and not the CEO's. This is true, but we believe that the impetus for bringing intraprise to a business should come from the very top, if possible. It's too controversial – think of all those dragons waiting out there to destroy it.

We feel that the best way for HR to foster intraprise within the business is to enthuse the CEO. However, there are steps that can be taken without top buy-in, which help greatly in creating the right environment as well as in delivering 'pure' HR benefits.

The Beermat Intrapreneurship Workshop can be presented as a standalone project. Given the poor success rate of most suggestion schemes, this can on its own make a big difference to general staff *morale*. This can be an excellent way to 'crack open' a door: once senior people see the quality of ideas and the improvement in morale, they are more likely to assent to larger intrapreneurial schemes.

Creating intraprise teams (and managing them using the tools described in this book) is in itself an excellent *training* vehicle, especially for *future leaders* – remember that person who described his intraprise as 'an MBA every day'. The challenge and the adventure associated with such schemes are often good tools to *keep* ▶▶

high-flyers motivated and, once word gets round, to help in the *attraction of talent* from other companies.

Some of the functions ideally carried out by an Enabling Venture Unit can be carried out by a switched-on HR department at little cost. Idea circulation, cultural events and the setting up of an interactive intranet are simple to establish and should almost run themselves, once they are going. These in turn will create a groundswell of intraprise within the company – a culture change that can have huge knock-on effects.

Beermat.biz

Chapter Eight: The Beermat Entrepreneur Process

This is the methodology that prepares ideas, gets them in front of the marketplace – with a sporting chance of success – and sorts out winners quickly. It works for entrepreneurs, and will do so for intrapreneurs.

With entrepreneurs 'out there', it can begin anywhere, but often seems to start in pubs – hence the name. The entrepreneur is sitting there with his or her friends, discussing a business idea. The discussion is heated: these people care about business, probably more than many slightly weary managers do. Ideas for new businesses are suggested: some foolish, most of them possibles. The process really takes off when one idea catches everyone's imagination. Comments like 'Now that *is* a good idea…' accompany it.

The individuals involved go away and think about it. If it still sounds a good idea next morning, they probably do some informal testing of it – the salesperson in the group chats to a few favourite customers in the relevant area, to see if they would be interested; the techie starts work on a prototype. When they reconvene, real progress has been made.

The same should happen internally. That's why informal networking activities, entrepreneur clubs and so on are so important. Ideas surface here and pass the very basic test of being taken seriously by intelligent and knowledgeable people.

The 'Original Beermat'

In the next pub session, our team fill in the 'Original Beermat'. We assume nobody has bought any paper, and the beermat happens to be to hand – luckily one of those ones with blank backs. There are three essential things you need to write on the mat:

★ elevator pitch

★ mentor (sponsor in a large organisation)

★ first customer.

Why these three things?

The *elevator pitch* is so important because it forces the team to concentrate on the essence of the business. Remember the Magic Question, 'Where's the pain?' The elevator pitch answers this question, and says how you are going to solve it. Ideally, the elevator pitch should include some form of differentiator – why should people buy the solution from you rather than from someone else?

The greatest elevator pitches are hugely evocative:

★ Bill Gates: 'Enable everyone to harness the power of personal computing.'

★ George Eastman (Kodak): 'A camera for everybody.'

★ AOL's Steve Case: 'Make the internet easy and make it fun.'

★ Montagu Burton (post-war British tailor): 'A three-piece suit for a week's wage.'

★ McKinsey & Co.: 'Management consultancy that's as professional as your law firm.'

★ Rolls-Royce's Silver Ghost: 'The best six-cylinder car in the world.'

★ Charles Merrill (founder of Merrill Lynch):'Bring Wall Street to Main Street.'

★ John D. Rockefeller at Standard Oil: 'Let the poor man have his cheap light.'

★ Aristide Boucicaut (founder of Bon Marché store): 'Democratise luxury!'

These are all highly ambitious – many aiming to create 'disruptive markets' by offering to everyone something that was once the prerogative of the rich or technologically savvy. (In our view, it's this capacity to create disruptive markets that makes capitalism superior to communism – but that's an aside!)

Less ambitious elevator pitches will allude back to the '10 per cent better/nicer/easier/cheaper' rule (see page 27). You can still build great businesses on these.

why should people buy the solution from you rather than from someone else?

Note that the pitches above are all one sentence long. This horrifies entrepreneurs, who love to go on endlessly about the fantastic new features of their amazing idea. But the whole point of the elevator pitch is that you get into the elevator and find yourself alone in there with Bill Gates. He presses seven, and you then have those floors to pitch him your idea. It does not allow for the elevator getting stuck.

It is a very good discipline for the intrapreneur and their team to sit down and work out exactly what their elevator pitch is – in one sentence. Hint: it's not an ad slogan. Good ad slogans should point to the key unique benefits of the product, but many just sound clever, or add 'branding' to undifferentiatable, commodity products (interesting stuff, but not what intraprise is about).

We have already talked about *sponsors*, so we will move on to the *first customer*.

We think this sets the right tone for the intraprise – from day one the team is thinking about who is actually going to buy the product.

Not 'who' in some general term (15–30-year-old redheads; men living north of Dewsbury; etc.), but a particular individual or institution.

The discipline of 'thinking of real live customers' seemed to vanish totally during the dot-com boom, resulting in immense value destruction.

who is actually going to buy the product.

Note that the customer can be internal. This is obviously true for a process idea at a Beermat Intrapreneurship Workshop session, but is also true for something an intrapreneur later intends to sell to the world. If there's an internal business unit that would clearly benefit hugely from the new product – sell it to them first.

If you can't think of a first customer, then you are likely to have a 'solution in search of a problem' on your hands. Reread Chapter Two and find another idea.

As we say in our talks, pencil the name of your first customer onto the beermat – you can only write it in pen when you actually have a cheque from this source.

The team

In the story of *The Beermat Entrepreneur* the nucleus of the team existed already, in the pub. The best possible start. However, the intrapreneur may be filling in that 'Original Beermat' on their own. If so, it is time to start building a team.

We have talked in Chapter Three about the people you need. A reminder – these are:

★ sponsor

★ foil (optional)

★ cornerstones

★ Dream Team.

The best way to get all of them is by personal contact. That is why great intrapreneurs are good networkers. They know a lot of people in the company; they know who's eager and free to join an intrapreneurial team, and (roughly) where their skills and passions lie.

We have covered this topic already and don't want to bang on about it. Just remember that, as in an enterprise 'out there', the team does not have to be full-time early on.

The seedling phase

This is when the new business consists of the intrapreneur plus the cornerstones (putting in as much time as they can). It may take time to recruit a full complement of cornerstones – but in the interests of creating a Balanced Business Team, this must be done. Keep networking; get your existing cornerstones networking. Many start-ups can get a long way as 'seedlings' – the phase ends when you start taking on extra people, who are no longer cornerstones (in practice, you may well have an administrator on board before the real recruiting drive begins, who will be a kind of 'honorary cornerstone').

During this time, the model of activity is:

★ get customer input

★ devise prototypes

   loop this until…

★ first actual sale

★ White Paper.

The looping process is very important. We've already discussed the importance of finding customer mentors – customers who will really engage with the project and help you get it right. They will do this because they like you and because the product has the potential to remove real, current 'pain' for them.

In an ideal world they would pay upfront for the prototype. This is the dream outcome for the cash-strapped entrepreneur. For the intrapreneur it is slightly less of a lifeline – remember, you are getting a load of stuff free at the moment. But ask anyway: it's a test of how bad the customer 'pain' is.

Your first sale should be a cause for major celebration. Celebration is a key part of life in the start-up: begin as you mean to go on.

The first sale should be written up in a White Paper. This is a description of how the sale went, including information such as:

★ what convinced the customer to buy

★ how it was delivered

★ the customer's experience of the product (good and bad)

★ changes you intend to make in the light of this.

Of special interest in the third section is anything *unexpected* that the customer found useful.

For entrepreneurs, this document has a dual function.

It is an internal memorandum to the team. It points out any shortcomings, so that you can remedy them next time. It also tells you exactly what the key benefits of your product are (or look likely to be). This may sound odd – shouldn't you know the key benefits to start with? – but remember Goldman's Law. You only think you know your key benefits. The market will tell you what they actually are.

Your White Paper can also be worked into a sales document, highlighting the good points of the customer's experience. This is by far the best sales collateral you can have – much better than any clever slogan or smart brochure. 'XYZ used our grommet and it worked really well.' Try working the story into a piece for the trade press. The trade press hates press releases of the 'New grommet launched by ABC Ltd' kind; it loves real case-studies where there's a story of a company having a problem and the new grommet actually solving it.

For the intrapreneur, the White Paper has a third use – within the corporation. Your supporters (CEO, sponsor, Enabling Venture Unit) will be delighted to hear of your success. Make sure they know about it (the CEO hasn't got time to read the whole paper, but a simple email announcing your first sale will cheer him or her up). The dragons will pretend to shrug it off – but it is a new weapon to be locked away in your armoury.

The paper will also prove an essential ally in a bid for allocations of time and funding. Having proven the concept, not just in theory but in practice – someone out there has paid for it and likes it – you should be looking to up the stakes. You should be wanting to spend more time on the project, and asking the company for this time. Some funding may be required for redesign in the light of customer comments and/or for financing the next phase of the product's roll-out. Yes, the perfect Beermat company funds from revenue, and we recommend this wherever possible, but some manufacturing plays may need some financial input at this point.

Note that the White Paper is not the end of the 'looping process'. You now know what one customer loves about the product. What about others? As you make the next sales, you should be aware that the product is still malleable. New customers may well say, 'Yes, your first customer has a big grommet problem, but ours is slightly different.' Adapt to fit their needs.

This process needs to be handled thoughtfully. You can't adapt to every customer requirement, unless you're delivering top-of-the-range, customised products. The point of being adaptable in early sales is to try and find out the 'real shape' of the market out there. Are there real, discrete groups of customers with similar (but different to other groups') needs? If so, what are the approximate relative sizes of these groups?

Ideally, you will find that the majority of customers have essentially similar 'pain' and can thus be served by a basic, core product. But it is wise to be aware of ancillary markets, people who also get benefits from the product, but in different ways. Once the core product is up and running, you can turn your attention to these other customers.

By all means get some mentoring from contacts in the marketing department, but in the end you and your team, especially the sales cornerstone, must be *the* experts in the markets for your products. Make it your business to develop a 'feel' for the marketplace – what it really needs; what it says it needs but actually won't pay for; who's really interested in new products and who just says they are.

When you have developed this awareness (hopefully after not too many sales) it's time to draw up the Real Business Plan.

You will of course have had to draw up Business Plans already, but they have been, essentially, helpful fictions. Now you have a clear enough idea of the size, structure and enthusiasm level of your market(s), it is time seriously to plan how you are going to attack those markets and win.

Note: the company may also be interested in 'Corporate Fit', if the intraprise dovetails with its own strategy. But don't be afraid to leave this out if there is little dovetailing: the strategy of the truly intrapreneurial company is to empower people like you to go out and create businesses (effectively creating micro-strategies, in your chosen area).

Alert readers of *The Beermat Entrepreneur* will note that this plan comes a little later in the process than for the start-up 'in the wild'. This is because most entrepreneurs need the discipline of a serious plan earlier than intrapreneurs do.

The Real Business Plan

1. **Intro**: elevator pitch; basic technology, production and delivery plan; revenue model.

2. **Market overview**:
   - ★ drivers
   - ★ main competition
   - ★ key customers.

3. **Sales plan**.

4. **Ops plan**. How and where production will take place: machines/space required. The same for delivery.

5. **Strategic assistance required**. What assets you are going to need from the parent company.

6. **Any external strategic alliances** you intend to form.

7. **People plan**. Probably the most important part of the whole thing. If you need to hire in new people, what sort of people and when? How will everyone's performance be measured?

8. **Financial projections**. These will be vaguer than standard corporate 'numbers'.

Beermat.biz

The model for the Real Business Plan should be whatever template you use in your company for such plans. If there are no such templates, then try the one above.

As with the White Paper, make sure all your allies in the corporation see the plan. If you can keep it from the dragons, do so – you don't want it coming back with charred edges – but it is impolitic to be seen to be preventing people from seeing your plans. Be subtle.

The sapling phase

The Real Business Plan should be a serious declaration of intent to 'go for it'. The business will now begin to grow faster, entering a new phase in its life. There may be a need for another round of funding, and for any time issues to be sorted out. Ideally, you and the team should be working full-time on the project now (certainly the entrepreneur, sales and delivery cornerstones should be).

You will start taking on people, moving beyond the Founding Team of entrepreneur plus cornerstones (plus, possibly, an administrator), to building the Dream Team. We've already talked about these essential people in Chapters Three and Four. They are great to have around, and they should inspire you to keep to your vision of a business unit that is passionate about what it does and fun to work in.

Life after 25

Some numbers do seem to have magic qualities – particularly when it comes to the numbers of people in an organisation. We've already spoken of our enthusiasm for the number five: the entrepreneur plus four cornerstones.

Beyond that lies another magic number. It's vaguer, between 20 and 30 people, and it's the point at which the small, growing business ceases being like a tribe or a sports team and begins to turn into a mini-corporate. It must be to do with the psychology of how many individuals we can really get to know, like and trust. Our ancestors probably roamed the African savannah in groups of about 25 adults.

Grow beyond 25 people, and strange things start happening to your business. You walk in one day and there's someone at a desk whom you don't recognise. When you were once delighted to be copied in on everyone's emails, suddenly it's become a chore. Your people start complaining they're not being listened to: you feel you're still trying your best, but there's just not enough time.

The solution, sadly, is to accept the change and introduce more structure. Your people should be having regular, formal assessments every six months. Are they? Have you got a full-time HR person? Maybe you don't need one with 25 people, but when it gets to 40 or 50… Are you still trying to get by on Word, Excel and the brilliant memory of your CFO's assistant?

For many entrepreneurs this change can be heartbreaking. Things just aren't such fun any longer! But it must be made.

So can the fun be preserved? We think it can – up to a point. It'll never be quite the same again, but you don't all have to rush off and buy suits and white shirts. ▶▶

If the company was a good place to work, that will be because it had a good corporate culture. This culture undoubtedly grew naturally, from a string of particularly good evenings down the pub, or from the wisecracks of one particularly funny team member, or from any of a hundred sources of that wonderfully indefinable and human thing called culture. It needs formalising now. If everyone went to the pub on Fridays, make sure that still goes on. Remind yourself of the mythology that has grown up in the business, and ensure it is passed on to new arrivals.

At The Instruction Set there were monthly awards: some serious, some silly, all of them hugely important for fostering team spirit. They kept these going even when the head count got beyond 100.

Keep recruitment a tribal thing for as long as possible. Potential employees of The Instruction Set met as many team members as possible as part of the interview process – and if any of the team got a bad feeling about them, the person did not join. Draconian? Ponderous? It was wonderfully effective: they lost a handful of people in their entire history.

What is not possible is to pretend nothing has changed: the 'Peter Pan' strategy. It can be disastrous. If you need a mental model to put you off the 'Peter Pan' approach, think of those embarrassing people in their forties who still pretend to be teenagers.

▶▶

Is there a magic number beyond 30? 150 people seems to be another point to stop and reflect. It was the point at which The Instruction Set was sold, and we have met other entrepreneurs who say that this is another milestone.

So if you are growing your company fast, don't be surprised if things suddenly seem less fun. Adapt to the change and you can keep that start-up spirit alive in your workplace. Up to a point.

Beermat.biz

Going for growth

Beyond about 25 people, the business changes its nature (see the box). The people you take on will be less 'tribal' than the Dream Teamers. They'll be ordinary, decent nine-to-five types, who do a good day's work, then head home to more important things. You will need a more formal, less charismatic style of management.

For the enterprise, there is often a choice to be made here. Do you really want to grow beyond 25? Particularly in upmarket services, there's a great living to be earned from serving existing customers superbly and working with people you really like and respect. Such outfits are often called 'boutiques'.

For the intraprise, the pressure to grow must be stronger. The 'choice to stay small' is a lifestyle choice taken by the business's owners. The intraprise is owned by the corporation, which is not in business to create great lifestyles for its people.

Once the intraprise is set on the growth path, the issue of 'sending in suits' will soon emerge, probably when the business gets to around 50–80 people. The Venture Unit should be in charge of this process – and should discharge that responsibility with delicacy and intelligence.

The intrapreneur and the cornerstones should be checked to see if they have made the transition from tribal, person-to-person leaders to more solid, process-following managers. In enterprises, cornerstones often 'burn out' at this point, or just become unsuitable. The finance cornerstone was happy watching costs and cashflow in the start-up; now a three-year plan is needed. The sales cornerstone enjoyed finding and talking to customers; now they sit at a desk managing a sales team. The delivery cornerstone was happiest making prototypes and adapting borrowed machinery; now there's a plan for a £1 million production line.

'Wild' entrepreneurs are the most erratic of all. Every VC we talk to says there nearly always comes a point when their dearest wish is to sideline the entrepreneur because they are sabotaging the growth of the company. While we usually defend entrepreneurs against criticism from VCs, the VCs do have a point here. *Intra*preneurs will probably be less erratic, but most of them are still not really big-company people, and would be more useful and happier back starting another business.

It is imperative that this is done on a case-by-case basis. If the cornerstones have made the transition to managers, then they must be kept there and allowed to grow with the business they founded. The moment someone in the Venture Unit (or anywhere) starts saying, 'There are more than 35 people in this new business unit, therefore the founders should be fired' is the moment bureaucracy starts regaining ground from intrapreneurialism.

A key job of the Venture Unit is to monitor the progress of *all* intrapreneurs and cornerstones, to keep watch that they are handling the '20 to 40' transition effectively, to give them assistance in making this transition and to step in only when things are going wrong.

In truth, the other cornerstones will know if someone is struggling, so if the Venture Unit make it their business to talk to all intrapreneurs and cornerstones, as well as sponsors and finance providers, they should gain a handle on this issue relatively easily. Finding and inserting the replacement may be more difficult, but must be done.

When the new unit gets very big – 150 is a psychologically important number to bear in mind – the question of spinning off arises. 'Going public' is a nightmare for most entrepreneurs: a bitter irony, as many of them dream of this day for years, little realising that it often leaves them with shares they can't sell and a host of regulators, analysts, institutional shareholders and bankers on their backs. Similarly, we think that a company focused on innovation should think twice before selling off successful ventures.

Ideally, the decision criteria should be cultural, not financial or even strategic. If the intraprise is largely staffed by people who have come from the company, then to sell them off would be to lose a valuable asset: loyalty. If they are largely outsiders, then a sell-off is less of a problem.

The other cornerstones will know if someone is struggling

If you decide the new unit must go, we are agnostic about which route. Flotation is almost impossible in the current market, but may be an option open to future readers; a trade sale often has strategic logic (but isn't your strategy to be as intrapreneurial as possible?); some kind of buy-out or other VC-funded deal is another option.

Just as we recommend successful start-ups to stay private, so our preferred route is to keep successful business units and to carry on watching them (and helping them) grow. But we accept this is a somewhat heretical view!

If you do keep the 'new' unit – now a business nearing the 200-employee level, remember – consider that it too has become a formal organisation. Within it, potential intrapreneurs are probably sitting at their desks, imagining. New products, new services, process improvements, new markets, new strategies – muttering as they do so, 'if only…' Two powerful, liberating words.

The magical circle of corporate regeneration has performed a complete but gentle revolution, and is about to start all over again.

'If only…'

The life-cycle of an intrapreneurial idea

Background research (often directed by pure curiosity)

Idea!

Talk to a few colleagues

Talk to a few customers

First major decision point: should we spend any more time on this? If so…

★ Find sponsor

★ Form a Founding Team

★ Rustle up prototype

★ Loop till first sale

★ White Paper

Second major decision point: should we spend a serious amount of time on this, and should we seek a seed 'bursary'?

★ Redesign if necessary

★ More sales

★ Discover real market breakdown

★ Design early models to suit each major market (or stick to major market if one clearly dominates)

★ Are customers happy with these?

★ Refine if necessary

★ Draw up Real Business Plan

Third major decision point: Founding Team to go full-time? Backers to inject more substantial amounts of capital?

★ Roll-out

★ Employ Dream Team

★ Incrementally improve product(s)

Fourth major decision point: stay small or 'go for growth'?

★ Take on employees

★ Formalise management structures

★ Keep close watch on intrapreneur and cornerstones – are they handling the change?

★ Competitors start trying to muscle in. How strong are your barriers?

Fifth major decision point: should the parent sell or retain the business?

🍺Beermat.biz

Conclusion

When the CEO got upstairs, she read through the plan for the Venture Unit and decided now was not the right time for it. She was sad to do so, as she felt that the company did need to return to its entrepreneurial roots. She avoided looking at the bust of Sir Ernest on her way out that evening.

But a few days later the HR director actually arrived at the same time as she did, and mentioned as they walked up the steps that he wanted a word with her. He'd got this idea for innovation – but not a costly one…

This plan was instituted exactly as set out in this book. The CEO decided on an 'upfront' approach. The result was a couple of stormy meetings and one resignation by someone she'd been wanting to get rid of for ages, but the rest of the company got behind the new initiative. More people than she expected put themselves forward as potential sponsors, several with particular projects in mind – a couple had already been working on them, in secret, and were delighted to be able to 'come out of the closet'.

Morale in the firm has improved. In the last year not a single individual on HR's list of 'high-flyers' has left, and they even managed to recruit a number of rising young talents from rivals.

The new businesses have had mixed success. Many fell at early hurdles, but several service initiatives have grown into small departments and are making profits. Two products are already on sale, one to an existing market and one to virgin (for the business) territory, where they have formed a strategic alliance with an experienced operator. One is in profit already; the other should be by the autumn. Several more are in the pipeline. A new internet-based business has already folded, but the losses were small.

At the same time the company has been doing well in its existing core markets. Customers and industry pundits have commented on a new, more positive approach from its people, and several 'incremental' innovations have gone down particularly well. Even the City appears to be noticing. In the last three months the company's share price has begun to outperform the industry index. Several analysts have upgraded the stock from 'Sell' to 'Hold', and in one case even 'Buy'.

The employee we saw getting up so unwillingly that Monday morning is not an intrapreneur – but he is a finance cornerstone for the second of the currently available products. He says that work is more exciting now than it has been for years.

The HR team are happy with the targets for general motivation, high-flyer retention and recruitment; and their director recently sat down with the CEO and produced a radically new list of potential replacements for her. Not that she plans to retire for a while, of course – not the way things are going now.

Appendix A: **Two Classic Intrapreneurs**

Art Fry

Art is the oft-quoted man behind the Post-it Note. He is an ideal role model for intrapreneurs, combining the entrepreneur's determination and eye for opportunity with excellent people and political skills. The last were particularly important: even in 3M, a company that prides itself on its intrapreneurial attitude, he had to fight hard, bend the rules and build alliances to see his product 'home'.

The Post-it story doesn't even begin with Fry. The semi-sticky gum on the back of the note was invented by Spencer Silver, a 3M scientist – who had no idea what to do with it. (Note the exploratory irrationality of the start of the process.) Being an enlightened company, 3M circulated the gum around to people, to see if they could come up with uses for it.

Fry, in the meantime, was singing in his church choir, and getting more and more annoyed by the fact that the bits of paper he used to mark hymns in his hymnal kept falling out. (Where was the pain? Not corporate: Fry was a 'frustrated consumer'.) He immediately saw the potential for the gum, which would stick to the page, but could then be peeled off without causing any damage.

There were some technical problems to be overcome – the level of stickiness had to be just right, and initially the new gum was too hit-and-miss. He spent ages talking to various people in various divisions of 3M (Fry was an assiduous networker) and eventually found someone who could solve these problems.

The next problem he encountered was internal: dragons. These were in the marketing department. Once the prototype was ready, Fry took the product to these people, and they did test marketing exercises on it. The result was poor. This is classic – emerging products do not fit the conventional marketing process, as the market is forming as the product emerges. Fry ended up working at night to create samples, then handed them out to people in the firm (in various formats: tape, labels, pads…). The result: people went crazy for the pads. Marketing had to give in.

Even so, the project nearly failed – a trial launch in four American cities yielded little success. But Fry's political skill (he had a range of sponsors, from his immediate boss to the company's President for International Operations) allowed him to keep the project alive. A second launch, in a smaller target zone but with more intensive promotion, was a huge success.

Twenty-five years on, we've still all got little yellow pads on our desks…

The Freeserve team

While the Post-it Note was driven by one brilliant intrapreneur, the story of Freeserve is about a team. Composed, of course, of intrapreneurially minded individuals. The originator of the idea was Ajaz Ahmed, a manager in a store of a subsidiary of the main company, Dixons. (So you don't have to be at the heart of things to be a great intrapreneur.) He saw early on that the parent company should launch an Internet Services Provider. The parent did not see this.

The next key players were John Pluthero and Mark Danby, 'fast-track' graduates in Dixons' new ideas unit. They teamed up with the persistent Ahmed, researched the market for an ISP – and couldn't come up with a revenue model. A fourth individual, external businessman Peter Wilkinson, came up with this. Wilkinson also created some great strategic alliances with outside suppliers (Planet Online would host the site, Energis provide telecoms, Lycos provide the material). All Dixons needed to do was make the sign-up CDs and stick them in their shops. Wilkinson's fantastic network proved crucial to the success of the enterprise – a reminder that, unlike the Post-it Note, some intraprises will only work if you ally with external players.

The project encountered dragons in the form of store managers, who were reluctant to have the discs being given away in their shops. But the team had done their politics well – Sir Stanley Kalms supported the project, and the managers had to stock them.

As with many entrepreneurial ventures, Freeserve was an instant success, amazing even the people who'd fought tooth and nail for it. Goldman's Law was at work!

Note, finally, that Freeserve was not the first ISP to offer free access to people. But it was the first to be promoted nationally, with a major national brand behind it. Such is the advantage the intrapreneur can have over the 'unsupported' entrepreneur.

And a memo to objectors who say that 'Intraprises are too small to make a real difference to the wealth of major companies'… Dixons' initial investment in Freeserve was £75,000, plus the time of the core team and a marketing budget once the discs were out for distribution in the shops. They later sold 20 per cent of the company for £300 million.

Appendix B: **A Model Intrapreneurship Programme**

The fundamental logic behind this programme is to make the process of intrapreneurship as similar to the process of entrepreneurship 'out there' as possible. This would seem an obvious thing to do, but actual Corporate Business Creation initiatives often become enmired in bureaucracy and cost a lot of money. 'Out there' most businesses start in a totally different way: start-ups are flexible and many start with no (or very little) capital.

There are three essential aspects to the programme: firstly, corporate buy-in; secondly, selection of the right individuals; thirdly, monitoring the progress of their projects. Some education between the second and third aspects is also useful.

Corporate buy-in

No intrapreneurship programme will work without two key things: CEO support and sponsors.

CEO support is self-explanatory: there will be enemies of the programme, and they will sabotage anything that is not championed right from the top.

Sponsors are senior managers who are prepared to act as mentors for intrapreneurs, providing advice, opening doors, and so on, and also keeping an eye on things from the company's point of view.

Intrapreneur selection

It is a fundamental tenet of this programme that the key to success is people. This is the case 'out there', where ideas are ten a penny, but good entrepreneurs are rare.

How do you make this selection? Up to a point, this sorts itself out. Ask for volunteers, and intrapreneurs will step forward.

Other selection methods include:

Intrapreneur audits. Explain the Beermat entrepreneur profile to long-standing middle managers, and ask them who they think would make good intrapreneurs. Also ask HR.

The Beermat Intrapreneurship Workshop. The audience are given a quick course in the Beermat model of entrepreneurship, then split into teams and asked to come up with – and present – new ideas for the company, in the form of an elevator pitch, a sponsor and a first customer.

Note that this can be targeted at new products/markets or simply at internal improvements (with the 'first customer' being an internal department) – or, of course, both. In most cases the ideas are excellent; often the best ones come from unexpected sources.

Psychological profiling. See pages 21–23 for material on this.

None of the above is sufficient on its own, but taken together they should produce a group of people with 'the right stuff'.

Education

We suggest that selected intrapreneurs be given a short reading list:

★ our own *The Beermat Entrepreneur*

★ *Intrapreneuring* by Gifford Pinchot III.

Monitoring progress

The early progress of an entrepreneurial idea can be broken down into three states, and exactly the same is true for an 'intrapreneurial' one.

Phase 1 – The Primal Soup (five tests)

First, the intrapreneur has to draw up their 'Original Beermat', outlining the *elevator pitch*, *mentor* and *first customer* for the idea. The elevator pitch is a clear, succinct statement of the benefit they are delivering, to whom, and why customers should go to them rather than anyone else. The first customer is notional – at the moment.

They also have to start attracting a team. Entrepreneurial teams usually begin with the entrepreneur plus a 'foil' and – ideally – one other cornerstone. (In the Beermat model, the entrepreneur needs four cornerstones around them, to 'ground' them and to carry out various specialist tasks such as finance, sales and ops.) At this stage the intrapreneur needs a foil and one other cornerstone. Among these must be someone with sales experience.

So, the business has filled in its 'Original Beermat' and has a team of an intrapreneur plus two cornerstones (one of whom is a sales specialist). It is ready to move on...

Phase 2 – The First Iteration (seven tests)

The business now needs an actual first customer and to deliver to that customer. So a prototype needs to be built (or service planned) and delivered. The point here is: a) to counter perfectionism, and b) to get revenue flowing in as soon as possible. Taking these in turn… Build a prototype that sort-of does the job. If the elevator pitch is strong enough – in other words, if there is a strong enough need out there for the product – customers will be delighted to have anything that even starts to have an effect. Ideally they will work with you to make it better, as they need it so badly. The point about revenue is self-explanatory. Beermat businesses fund from revenue as far as possible (which is often totally possible, even for manufacturing).

When the first product has been delivered, has been used by the customer and has had glitches ironed out – so the customer understands how to use it, and the producer understands what the customer really needs *and* has gone some way to providing that – both sides should sit down and write a 'White Paper'. This is the 'story of the product's implementation': what went wrong, what proved invaluable, what insights have been gained from the experience. If there was a lot of learning involved, the WP is invaluable to enable the team to go back and make changes.

The process probably needs to be iterated until things run smoothly, at which point the WP is a perfect sales document. But for the purposes of exiting this phase, all that is necessary is for the story of the first sale to be written up in WP form!

The business now needs a full complement of cornerstones. Four is the ideal number, creating a balance. These should be finance, sales, ops and either innovation or (if the intrapreneur is the innovator) an expert in the most difficult area that the business faces. These four cornerstones plus the intrapreneur are the board and the driving force of the new business.

Note that cornerstones do not have to be full-time to start off with.

So we have seven more tasks fulfilled. A prototype has been built, and delivered. A customer has written out a cheque, and used the delivered product. A White Paper has been written about the experience. Two more cornerstones have joined the team.

Phase 3 – Finding Your Feet (six tests)

This phase begins once major teething troubles have been sorted out, ideally with the first customer, but in reality maybe with two or three customers. White Papers have been written for each iteration, until one exists that is the tale of a successful implementation with no (or virtually no) problems. The third phase can now begin (so there is a possible gap between Phase 2 and Phase 3 while the product is iterated: customer uses; problems; problems ironed out; WP written; customer uses new version…).

The task is now to 'scale' this. The next target is ten more customers, all happy with what they have received. (Thus two tests – first, securing ten paying customers; second, ending up with ten happy customers. It is, of course, possible to pass the first but fail the second; the testing goes on until there are ten happy customers!)

A further test is a Market Segmentation Analysis. Does the product sell into different markets? Note that a market is here defined functionally, by the core benefit that the customer derives from the product.

In terms of the team, the business should be employing 'Dream

Team' people (eager young employees). At least two should be on board, and be clearly happy and motivated.

Finally, the business needs to draw up a 'Real Business Plan'. Any previous business planning has been guesswork. Now the business should have a clear idea of the 'clout' it carries in the marketplace – how passionately do customers want what they deliver? – and whether the product can be made and delivered profitably.

So in this phase there are six tests. Ten customers; ten happy customers; the 'contours' of the market understood; two Dream Teamers employed and happy; and a Real Business Plan drawn up.

Beyond this point, the business must move on from its entrepreneurial roots – just as start-ups do, into a more structured phase. Many entre- and intrapreneurs lose interest at this point and go in search of new challenges.

Appendix C: The Public-Sector Entrepreneur

This book has been set in a corporate context, as it is where we have our roots. However, its message is not restricted to the private sector. The modern public sector faces challenges that are in many ways similar to that of the corporate sector in search of self-renewal.

No, there is not the danger of rapid extinction that faces the static company: Anyshire County Council will not be 'driven out of business' if it does not innovate. But behind this truism lurk a number of threats that smart public servants are well aware of.

Society is changing ever faster, becoming more diverse: ethnically, culturally, in the lifestyles we choose – in every possible way. This unending social change is meat and drink to commercial entrepreneurs, who are forever developing new products and services to meet these changes. But it is a challenge to public bodies as well. Unless they change as fast as society, they will be falling behind in the quality of service they provide. Remaining static – 'We've always done things this way' – is no more an option for public bodies than it is for private ones.

At the same time, users' expectations of public services are getting higher and higher. The private sector is responsible for this: we're getting accustomed to stunning service from the best private companies. So not only is society getting harder and harder to serve, but people expect more.

Cynics say that this may be the case, but since there is no pressure on public bodies analogous to that put on businesses by the market, nothing need happen. They are wrong. We live in a democracy, so there is political, not commercial, pressure. If public services are seen to be failing to meet the standards expected of them, voters will exert massive pressure through the ballot box. This pressure is not to be underestimated: there is a political opposition out there, relentlessly looking for failings in public service to use as political ammunition.

Public bodies have no choice but to innovate. Exactly like big corporations, they cannot do this by committee. Instead, they must empower their people to experiment, to ask the entrepreneur's Magic Question – 'Where's the pain?' – and to develop and test solutions. And to fail, learn, rethink, try again.

Essential examples of public-sector pain are exactly the same as those for large organisations. Are resources being wasted internally? Are there groups of customers being appallingly served? A special problem for government: are agencies hard at work duplicating each other's efforts? One very entrepreneurial public servant we spoke to recently created a group of like-minded individuals from different departments to address this problem. We need more people like her.

We believe it is a myth that public-sector people lack the 'oomph' to create change. Some clearly do – Sir Humphrey Appleby rang many bells – but so do many people in corporations. Intrapreneurship is not for everybody. We believe there is a critical mass of able and imaginative people in most public-sector organisations who could make a real difference – and who will make a difference, given the opportunity and the right methodology.

Of course, the political nature of public-service work makes life tougher for public-sector intrapreneurs: the media make it hard to 'experiment but fail' in the way corporate intrapreneurs can do. But this extra pressure must be lived with: there is no better way of bringing about the change that public bodies need than by empowering intrapreneurs. As with private companies, a CEO figure who roundly defends his or her intrapreneurs – in the case of public bodies, against external as well as internal enemies – is essential to the process.

Appendix D: **A Basic Reading List**

There are many books on the subject of innovation and intrapreneurship: this is a recommended selection.

The classic text on intrapreneurship is Gifford Pinchot's *Intrapreneuring*. Scores of management fads have risen and fallen since this was first published back in the 1980s, but this splendid volume remains as fresh and relevant as ever.

Our own *The Beermat Entrepreneur* explains the entrepreneurs' methodology, which we recommend intrapreneurs take into the corporate workplace. It also contains 'war stories' from Mike's start-up ventures, particularly The Instruction Set.

Public-sector intrapreneurs should read *Civic Entrepreneurship* by Charles Leadbeater and Sue Goss. This short book combines an excellent discussion of the challenges with some great stories of inspirational individuals who've gone out and changed things in the public sector. It has the added advantage of being downloadable free from the website of its publishers, the 'think tank' Demos.

Clayton Christensen's *The Innovator's Dilemma* is a superb study of 'disruptive' technologies – ideas that work their way from despised, niche markets to mainstream ones. The killer point is that big corporations miss these challenges not through stupidity, but because they are doing their jobs well – listening to existing customers, incrementally improving products. Only the intrapreneur, who takes a fresh view of the marketplace and how to serve it, can break the 'spell of existing excellence' and take on disruptors.

Professor Christensen has recently followed this up with *The Innovator's Solution*, which is equally excellent, albeit a little harder to read. If you get bogged down, leap to Chapters Seven and Eight: classic Beermat ideas, restated in the language of Harvard Business School.

Gary Hamel's *Leading the Revolution* is on the surface an antithesis to what we argue, with its Maoist revolutionary fervour. But scrape away the excessive expectations for dot-coms and, er, Enron, and the author is spot-on. He understands that in order to succeed at innovation, companies must have a methodology for 'failing quickly, cheaply and often', for learning from those experiments and going on to win. His enthusiasm for innovation and innovators is a tonic, especially for those times when the dragons get a bit too close for comfort.

The Change Masters by Rosabeth Moss Kanter is another classic book that takes a slightly different view from ours – in the other direction: her change masters are a little less maverick than Beermat intrapreneurs. But fundamentally she is writing about the same process, and provides many valuable insights.

Weird Ideas that Work by Robert I. Sutton takes a radical perspective on almost all aspects of corporate life. It's probably more relevant to Silicon Valley than UK manufacturing – but precisely for that reason it's a stimulating read.

Sutton also co-wrote *The Knowing-Doing Gap*, with Jeffrey Pfeffer. This book is particularly good on the dangers of pointless cleverness, and a reminder that business – for intrapreneurs as well as big corporates – is ultimately about execution.

Andrew Hargadon's *How Breakthroughs Happen* shows how innovation is a team business, a slow business, and comes from broad as well as deep thinking.

Rembrandts in the Attic by Kevin Rivette and David Kline covers the subject of IP and its strategic value.

Harvard Business Review has produced some excellent articles on innovation. Recommended recent pieces are:

★ 'Radical Change, the Quiet Way' by Debra E. Myerson, (October 2001)

★ 'The Discipline of Innovation' by Peter Drucker (reprinted August 2002)

★ 'Serving the World's Poor Profitably' by C.K. Prahalad and Allen Hammond (September 2002)

★ 'Bottom-feeding for Blockbuster Businesses' (= radical trading down) by David Rosenblum, Doug Tomlinson and Larry Scott (March 2003)

★ 'Luxury for the Masses' (= trading up) by Michael J. Silverstein and Neil Fiske (April 2003)

★ 'Innovating for Cash' by James P. Andrew and Harold L. Sirkin (September 2003)

The July/Aug 2004 Review focused on 'Top-line growth', and featured reprints of some classic articles: 'Marketing Myopia' by Theodore Levitt, 'Value Innovation' by W. Chan Kim and Renée Mauborgne and 'The Middle Manager as Innovator' by Rosabeth Moss Kanter.